KNOWLEDGE AND REALITY
A Comparative
Study of Quine
and
Some Buddhist Logicians

KNOWLEDGE AND REALITY
A Comparative Study of Quine and Some Buddhist Logicians

KAISA PUHAKKA

MOTILAL BANARSIDASS
Delhi :: Patna :: Varanasi

ⓒMOTILAL BANARSIDASS
Indological Publishers & Booksellers
Head Office : BUNGALOW ROAD, JAWAHARNAGAR, DELHI-7
Branches : CHOWK, VARANASI-1 (U.P.)
ASHOK RAJPATH, PATNA-4 (BIHAR)

ISBN 0-8426-0804-4

First Edition : *Delhi*, 1975
Price Rs 25.00

Printed in India
BY SHANTILAL JAIN, AT SHRI JAINENDRA PRESS, BUNGALOW ROAD, JAWAHAR
NAGAR, DELHI-7 AND PUBLISHED BY SUNDARLAL JAIN, FOR MOTILAL
BANARSIDASS, BUNGALOW ROAD, JAWAHAR NAGAR, DELHI-7.

To
RAMA

FOREWORD

Detailed and systematic work in the field of comparative philosophy is still in its infancy. And despite the oft-heard platitude that the globe is constantly shrinking and that the need for dialogue and exchange between different traditions is greater than ever before, philosophers of each tradition, holding that theirs is the only true and worthy philosophy, either remain in a state of comfortable ignorance of other traditions or display towards these an attitude of contempt and hostility—an attitude based on nothing more than popular cliches, journalistic vignettes, or the blind and dogmatic pronouncements of the great and mighty of their own traditions.

Nevertheless, there have been signs of encouragement. Thus in the recent years have appeared excellent translations of important and not easily accessible Indian and Chinese philosophical classics—for example, D. Sharma's *The Differentiation Theory of Meaning in Indian Logic* and A.C. Senape McDermott's *An Eleventh-Century Buddhist Logic of 'Exists'*. Another line of progress in comparative philosophy consists of the analytical study and critique of specific problems. Ms. Puhakka's work falls in this group.

Ms. Puhakka examines the logical, epistemological, and ontological doctrines of Dignāga and Dharmakīrti on the one hand and of W. V. Quine on the other. It is well-known, that Quine had shaken one of the pillars of Western philosophical tradition by showing the untenability of a sharp line of demarcation between analytic and synthetic statements. Ms. Puhakka shows that a position similar to Quine's obtains in the writings of the Buddhist logicians mentioned above, although for reasons not entirely similar to the ones behind Quine's arguments. With deep insight, she argues that the analytic-synthetic distinction is based on two more fundamental distinctions, namely, meaning-reference and substance-attribute. Ms. Puhakka provides convincing arguments to the effect that the Buddhist logicians' rejection of substance ontology naturally leads to a rejection of any claim to the ultimacy of the above dichotomies and therewith of the analytic-synthetic distinction.

She then examines Quine's notion of existence—to exist is to be a value of a bound variable—and shows that this way of dealing with existence is grounded in substance ontology, contrary to the general tenor of Quine's ontology. She explains this anomaly by distinguishing first-order and second-order ontological statements and universal and particular illusion—distinctions which she formulates in the light of her interpretation of the writings of the Buddhist logicians.

In addition to these highly original arguments, Ms. Puhakka has some interesting things to say about language, negation, and reality, from a comparative point of view.

One last remark : I do not believe that Ms. Puhakka claims that her treatment of Quine and the Buddhist logicians is beyond dispute. I am sure there is plenty of room for disagreement in interpretation and therewith on the conclusions. If so, Ms. Puhakka should be commended for bringing into focus important and interesting philosophical problems and suggesting solutions. Needless to say, any book that accomplishes this will have been more than successful.

Ramakrishna Puligandla
Professor of Philosophy
The University of Toledo

Toledo, Ohio
December 18, 1974

PREFACE

A knowledgeable student of comparative philosophy whom I may be privileged to have as my reader is likely to be struck by the conspicuous omission of historical details concerning the Buddhist (as well as Western) tradition in my work. I am fully aware of the fact that I have not treated all, perhaps no even most, of the prominent Buddhist logicians who flourished in the various schools from the Sarvāstivādins of the Hīnayāna tradition to the Prāsaṅgikas of the Mahāyāna tradition. But then the present work is not intended to be a compendium of either Buddhist or Western logic but rather a comparative analysis of certain aspects of these traditions as they bear upon some central problems of logic and ontology.

These problems arise whenever one attempts to inquire into the relation between language and reality. The very posing of the problem of the relation between language and reality presupposes the meaning-reference distinction, which is the basis of the analytic-synthetic distinction; for, as is well-known since Kant, an analytic statement is characterized as one which could be certified solely on the basis of *meanings*, whereas a synthetic statement requires a consideration of not only meanings but also states of affairs in the world—*referents*. Although the problem of the analytic-versus-synthetic has occupied a central place in Western philosophy and has been widely discussed, it has been scarcely dealt with from the point of view of non-Western traditions, for example, the Indian. The aim of the present work, then, is to approach this problem in the light of the writings of certain Buddhist logicians on language, reality, meaning, and reference. In order to gain a deeper understanding of the problem, I have undertaken a comparative treatment of it. Given the immensity of the logico-philosophical writings in the Indian tradition, no one can hope to treat the problem taking into account a large number of thinkers. For this reason, I have chosen to limit my discussion to Dignāga, Dharmakīrti, and Ratnakīrti who, in my judgment, had most important things to say on the problems at hand. It goes without saying that others may have dealt with different thinkers, but it is only appropriate that in critical studies, as distinguished from historical ones, problems determine the choice of writers to be considered and not the other way around.

Much valuable work has been done in making available important Buddhist texts in translations from Pali and Sanskrit and, more recently, from Chinese and Tibetan sources. Such work makes it possible to go beyond broad historical surveys to concentrated investigations of specific problems from a comparative standpoint. While first-hand knowledge of the literature of the various traditions is certainly necessary for any successful undertaking of comparative study, it is only when such knowledge is brought to bear upon the ideas, beliefs, and presuppositions of one's own tradition that the precious goal of comparative study—the widening of horizons and the emergence of novel perspectives—can be realized. The present work is offered to the scholars of comparative philosophy as a modest contribution toward this goal.

I wish to take this opportunity to express my gratitude to my mentor, Professor Ramakrishna Puligandla, whose spirit and skill as philosopher and dialectician have been a source of inspiration and encouragement throughout my student years. I am thankful to him for arousing in me interest in comparative philosophy and for suggesting the topic of the present work. Special thanks are due to Professor Douglas Daye for his expert help and advice in the writing of this book. I also wish to thank Professors Michael Bradie and Thomas Mayberry for their constructive criticisms and comments. Ms. Kay Wenzel deserves special mention and appreciation for efficient, meticulous, and elegant typing of the manuscript. Any faults that may yet remain, however, are entirely mine.

K. Puhakka

CONTENTS

I

INTRODUCTION

For a long time it was a general belief among philosophers in the West that language and reality are intimately connected with each other. There was of course no unanimous agreement as to how they were connected; but at least this much seems to be admitted by all: the presuppositions of knowledge and the fundamental laws of thought are grounded in reality and such grounding constitutes an adequate basis for their validity.

Lest these observations be construed as unfounded, they will be documented by some examples. To begin with Plato, the nature and function of language and its relation to reality are discussed in *Cratylus*, among other dialogues. To be sure, it is hard to determine what exactly Plato's conclusions, if any, concerning a philosophical problem are. Nevertheless, it seems possible to indicate, no matter how sketchily, that Plato was more inclined toward some views than others. Thus discussing names (and through them predication and essences) Socrates observes:

> Then, Hermogenes, I should say this giving of names can be no such light matter as you fancy, or the work of light or chance persons. And *Cratylus is right in saying that things have names by nature*, and that not every man is an artificer of names, but he only who looks to the name which each thing by nature has, and is able to express the true forms of things in letters and syllables.

To which Hermogenes, the conventionalist, responds by saying:

> I cannot answer you, Socrates, but I find a difficulty in changing my opinion all in a moment, and I think that I would be more readily persuaded if you would show me what this is which you term the natural fitness of names.

And Socrates replies as follows:

> My good Hermogenes, I have none to show. Was I not telling you just now—but you have forgotten—

> that I knew nothing, and was I not proposing to share the inquiry with you? But now that you and I have talked over the matter, a step has been gained, for *we have discovered that names have by nature a truth*, and that not every man knows how to give a thing a name.[1]

The following quotation from H. S. Thayer further supports the contention that Plato held that language reflects reality:

> The SOPHIST and CRATYLUS reveal *Plato's conviction that there is a vital link between language and the world.* There is the suggestion, which time and again has proved of fascination to philosophers, of a language evolved from a set of simple and primitive names— these being the names of the most simple and ulti- mate constituents of the world. Plato considers several of these languages and several ways in which the use and structure of statements has a relation to the structure of nature and Being. All this is not to be wondered at if we look at things through Plato's eyes, for language, too, is a part of nature and *a reflection of Being....*For Plato, then, language is a functional thing, an instrument. What is its ergon? The vacuous reply would go : the function of language is what it alone can do or do best. But filled-in, this means as Plato says : language is an instrument for conveying information about and making distinctions concerning reality (ousia). A language that functions well will be supervised in its construction by the man who knows its function. If language is to be able to express the "nature" (physis) and Forms of things, it is the dialectician, Plato's philosophic hero, who guides its construction, for he is the true user of language.[2]

One last point with regard to Plato. If according to the Theory of Ideas, Ideas are Being (reality), then one wonders whether

---

1. *The Collected Dialogues of Plato*, ed. E. Hamilton and H. Cairns, Pan- theon Books, N.Y., 1961, P. 429. Italics added.

2. H. S. Thayer, *Plato's Republic; Interpretation and Criticism*, ed. A. Sesonske, Wadsworth Publishing Co., Inc., Belmont, Calif., 1966. pp.38-39. This article originally appeared in *The Philosophical Quarterly*, Vol.14, 1964. Italics added.

Plato is not in some sense claiming not a mere correspondence but identity between thought and reality. But this point should perhaps not be pressed because the status of the Ideas in Plato is much disputed and controversial. It should be added, however, that although objections may be raised against interpreting the Ideas as thought, it is not at all clear as to what else they could be.

Aristotle says in the METAPHYSICS: "There is a science which investigates being qua being and the attributes which belong to this in virtue of its own nature." Such a science is philosophy, which "will examine not only the substances but also their attributes," together with "the truths which are in mathematics called axioms." The latter refer in particular to the first principles both of the syllogism and being qua being. Put differently, the philosopher is concerned with the first principles of being and demonstration. "Evidently then it belongs to the philosopher, i.e., to him who is studying the nature of all substance, to inquire also into the principles of syllogism." These principles are not peculiar to any particular science but are rather "the most certain principles of all things." Clearly indicative of the dual status of the principle of contradiction, are Aristotle's statements of it in two versions, the logical and the ontological, respectively: "that everything must be affirmed or denied; and that a thing cannot at the same time be and not be."[1] The point of all these quotes is that Aristotle believed that being qua being can be studied through logic and language and that logical principles are not arbitrary and conventional (nor are they merely laws of thought) but are grounded in the very nature of Being. The following observation by J.H. Randall supports this interpretation of Aristotle on the relation between language and reality:

> No, we can be said to "know" a thing only when we can
> state in precise language what that thing is, and why
> it is as it is. Knowledge and language are a flowering
> of the world, an operation of its power to be under-
> stood and expressed. *The Greek language, Aristotle is
> convinced*—somewhat naively, we moderns think—*is a*

---

1. *The Basic Works of Aristotle*, ed. R. McKeon, Random House, New York 1941, pp. 731-36.

perfect expression of the world's intelligibility. The structure of the Greek language and structure of the world are ultimately the same, because the Greek language is a natural instrument for knowing and expressing the world's structure. This view too is doubtless naive. But is it really more naive than our modern conviction that the structure of mathematics and the structure of the world are the same ?[1]

It is indeed of interest to note that among contemporary Western philosophers Morris Cohen and Ernest Nagel hold, like Aristotle, that the so-called laws of thought are not only laws of thought but also of Being. Thus after stating both the propositional and ontological versions of the law of identity, contradiction, and excluded middle, Cohen and Nagel say that the ontological version is "an obvious counterpart of the propositional version" and that "it expresses, perhaps even more clearly, that their subject matter is certain *general or generic traits of all things whatsoever*," and conclude that "as principles of being, logical principles are universally applicable" and "as principles of inference, they must be accepted by all, on pain of stultifying all thought."[2]

Leibniz accepts the correspondence theory of truth when he writes:

> Let us content ourselves with seeking truth in the correspondence of propositons in the mind with the things in question. It is true that I have also attributed truth to ideas in saying that ideas are true or false; but then I mean in reality the truth of propositions affirming the possibility of the object of the idea. In the same sense we can say also that a being is true, that is to say the proposition affirming its actual or at least possible existence.[3]

1. J. H. Randall, Jr., *Aristotle*, Columbia U. Press, New York, 1962, p. 7. Italics added. It may be mentioned that Professor Komer also is of the view that"According to Aristotle the principles of logic,in particular the laws of contradiction and excluded middle, are also ontological truths." (S. Korner, *What is Philosophy?* The Penguin Press, London, 1969, p. 182).

2. M. R. Cohen and E. Nagel, *An Introduction to Logic and Scientific Method*, Harcourt Brace and Co., New York, 1936, pp. 185-6.

3. Leibniz, *New Essays Concerning Human Understanding*, tr. A.G. Lanley, Lasalle, Illinois, 1949, p. 452.

With respect to Hegel, it is to belabor the obvious even to mention that logic and metaphysics (ontology) are one and the same. Thus the categories of his logic are the Absolute. The Idea, which is the culminating category, is the Absolute. "And the Absolute is not a mysterious something to which the categories being, substance, cause, etc, apply. The Absolute *is* the categories . . . And the categories, too, are on the one hand, *our* mental forms, while on the other hand they are objective entities, and as such are the Absolute."[1] Further "It (thought) knows that what is *thought, is,* and that what *is,* only *is* insofar as it is a thought."[2]   All this is summed up in the famous Hegelian dictum that the real is the rational and the rational is the real. Thus Hegel identifies knowing and being; and insofar as he claims that knowing can only be through his categories, the inescapable conclusion is that for Hegel the structure of language and thought are indeed the same as that of Reality.

One of the consequences of Kant's "Copernican revolution" was the reversal of the traditional conception of the relation between language and reality. It was no longer believed that thought and the expression of thought simply represent reality. That is, thought now became constitutive of reality. The modern interpretation of the Kantian view is even more radical: reality is no more and no less than the form given to it by language. As a consequence, the presuppositions of knowledge and the fundamental laws of thought could no longer be justified by appeal to reality. However, since these were regarded as constitutive of reality itself, they could not be challenged or criticized. For one would have to step outside of reality into some other standpoint to criticize them. But this is obviously impossible. Once the possibility of criticism is thus eliminated, the need for proof or justification is not felt.[3]

But whether pre-Kantian or post-Kantian, Western philosophical traditions have in general held firm to the view that

1. W. T. Stace, *The Philosophy of Hegel,* Dover, New York, 1955, p. 77.

2. *Hegel's Phenomenology of Mind,* tr. William Wallace, Clarendon Press, Oxford. 1894, p. 465.

3. With perhaps the single exception of Husserl in recent philosophy, See Edmund Husserl, *Formal and Transcendental Logic,* tr. Dorion Cairns, Martinus Nijhoff, The Hague, 1969.

there are no differences between reality and our conceptualizations about it; and even if it were true that there were some differences, *that* would make no difference to us. As Wittgenstein puts it, "The limits of my language are the limits of my world."[1] Thus,

> The large number of metaphysical, epistemological, ethical and other philosophical books written by Western thinkers from the time of Plato to the present attest to the fact that, with some reservations, Western philosophers have believed language to be an adequate medium for the communication of their philosophical beliefs about the world.[2]

The possibility that reality may be entirely different from and beyond the reach of our conceptualizations about it has never been seriously entertained in the mainstream of Western philosophy.

To be sure, there are thinkers, both past and present, who have doubted or even denied the ability of language and conceptual thought to reveal all aspects of reality. But even in the case of these thinkers, it is the adequacy, not the appropriateness, of conceptual thought that is usually called into question. The religious thinkers of the past, following St. Augustine, yielded to faith in the face of the incomprehensible, but as theologians they persisted in the search for understanding faith and explaining the unexplainable.[3] Thus it was the sense of the mysterious rather than the mystical that filled the minds of the theologians as they reached the limits of conceptual thought. While the mystical signalizes silence and cessation of the need to conceptualize, the mysterious demands answers and cries for solutions to be delivered, if not by man then perhaps by God. Many of those who resisted faith and tenaciously pursued the path of knowledge and Reason ended their journey in paradoxes, dilemmas, and finally, the sense of absurdity which has been the central concern of modern Existentialists:

1. Ludwig Wittgenstein, *Tractatus Logico-Philosophicus*, tr. D. F. Pears & B. F. McGuinness, The Humanities Press, N. Y., : 1963, p. 115.

2. H. Rosemont Jr., "The Meaning is the Use; Koan and Mondo as Linguistic Tools of the Zen Masters." *Philosophy East & West*, April 1970, p. 111.

3. William Barrett, *Irrational Man : A Study in Existential Philosophy*, a Doubleday Book, New York, 1962, p. 97.

The feeling and experience of absurdity arises out of the ways of knowing which man has traditionally had at his disposal and consequently his inability to obtain self-knowledge on the one hand, and knowledge of the world as a whole and the transcendent on the other. Thus, despite his yearning for knowledge which is both infinite and infallible, man's knowledge is finite, bounded by the unknown, and even within its limited sphere plagued with uncertainty. Man is overcome by the sense of absurdity when, approaching the limits of his knowledge, he is unable to transcend them.[1]

To repeat: Rational knowledge (and sometimes its counterpart, irrational faith) has been the vehicle by means of which Western men have approached reality. Although the inadequacy of conceptual knowledge has occasionally been felt, the notion that such knowledge might be a hindrance, a veil that actually conceals reality, has been alien to the theologian, the rational philosopher, and the apostle of the irrational alike.

The purpose of the present inquiry is to examine a philosophy which grows out of a tradition in many ways different from that of the West. The greatest difference between the two traditions lies in the fact that the former, unlike the latter, subscribes to the belief that conceptual knowledge does not depict reality. It is not just that some misguided and defective conceptual systems fail to correctly represent reality, but that all systems fail to do so. The philosophy in question is the school of Buddhist logicians called 'Vijñānavāda,' which flourished from around 400 A.D. to 1050 A.D. Among the chief exponents and commentators of this school were Dignāga (400 A.D.), Dharmakīrti (c. 550 A.D.), Dharmottara (800 A.D.), and Ratnakīrti (1050 A.D.). The Buddhist logicians subscribe to a double-standard of reality: on the one hand, there is the reality which is not an object of conceptual activity and empirical knowledge and hence about which nothing can be conveyed through thought and language; and on the other hand there is the reality which is the object of empirical know-

---

1. Ramakrishna Puligandla and Leena Kaisa Puhakka, "The Challenge of the Absurd," *Journal of Thought*, vol. 5, no. 2, 1970, p. 101.

ledge and which is known through experience and described
through language. However, contrary to what the term seems
to suggest, 'double-standard of reality' does not mean that there
are two numerically distinct realities. Rather, there is only
one reality which is looked at from two different points of view:
the one non-conceptual, direct apprehension by yogic intuition
(yogipratyakṣa) and the other conceptual-empirical knowledge (vijñāna).

Men have always found it much easier to recognize similarities than to understand differences between their own ways
of thinking and those of others. This is only natural since the
ability to understand differences presupposes a wider world-
view than that provided by one's own community, while the
recognition of similarities does not require venturing beyond
the familiar territory. Thus comparative studies in the philosophies of divergent cultural traditions often make the assumption
that the discovery of similarities and uniformities is more pro-
fitable and more enlightening than the acknowledgement of
genuine differences. Consequently, where the overlap between different world-views ends, there comparative studies
should also end. On this view of comparative study, it would
be tempting to ignore the importance which the Buddhists attach
to the double-standard of reality and reject the non-conceptual
reality on grounds that it is mysterious, unintelligible, and ins-
pired by religious sentiment, or simply on grounds that, whatever its nature and characteristics, nothing can be said about
it on the Buddhist's own admission (or on the ground that the
Western rational tradition has never needed to resort to the
non-conceptual, and if Buddhism is to be rational, it too can
do without the non-conceptual). Although such an approach
may be plausible on the level of everyday discourse, concerns
and pursuits—the Buddhists would be the first to admit this—it
is far from adequate on another level where the foundations of
all discourse and knowledge are in question. The presuppositions of knowledge and the fundamental laws of thought pres-
cribe the correct modes of thinking and knowing and thereby
prohibit alternatives to such modes of thinking and knowing.
But in so doing they draw the line between the conceptual and
the non-conceptual, the thinkable and the unthinkable. How
the presuppositions are expressed and the laws formulated,

what their status is, and how they are justified all depends on how the conceptual is related to the non-conceptual.

The views of the Buddhist logicians concerning the origin and justification of knowledge differ in some important respects from all those views and theories which in some way or other assume that in the last analysis knowledge and reality coincide. The Buddhist analysis discloses the common underlying presuppositions of the multitudinous and apparently divergent theories of knowledge and reality conceived and expounded in the Western philosophical tradition. In the light of the Buddhist theories of knowledge and reality, these presuppositions may be subjected to questioning, criticism, and review which only the availability of a radically different viewpoint makes possible.

Three interelated sets of presuppositions underlie all theories of knowledge and reality which are based on the belief that conceptual knowledge depicts non-conceptual reality. First, it is assumed that at least some words in the language through which knowledge is conveyed directly refer to objects in the extra-linguistic world which is the object of knowledge. Such words provide the bridge between the conceptual and non-conceptual.

Second, attempts to clarify the relationship between the conceptual and non-conceptual have given rise to the distinctions between 'meaning' and 'reference' on the one hand and between 'universal' and 'particular' on the other. Philosophers in the West have generally agreed that there is a connection on the one hand between 'meaning' and 'universal' and on the other, between 'reference' and 'particular.' But whether universals have anything to do with reference or particulars with meaning is an issue which has divided the Western philosophical tradition into the platonic and anti-platonic camps. In any case, the almost unanimous acceptance of the first two relationships has supported and left virtually unchallenged the belief that the dichotomies themselves, between meaning and reference and between universal and particular, correspond to some fundamental feature of reality. Underlying such a belief is the adherence to a substance ontology. For in order that a connection can be established between a word and its referent, the latter must consist of a distinct entity which endures at least through some length of time. All Western theorists

of meaning and reference have invariably subscribed to an ontology of such distinct entities. Whether these are considered
to be physical objects or just objects of sense-experience, as
long as they are capable of identification and differentiation
from other entities, events, and processes, they furnish the necessary basis for fixity and reference.

Third, the meaning-reference dichotomy is closely associated with another dichotomy which is the cornerstone of much of
Western philosophy, namely, the analytic-synthetic distinction.
Although at first sight the two dichotomies may seem unrelated
to one another, they not only have their common basis in substance ontology but also one logically implies the other. Thus
if extra-linguistic entities are in principle separable from linguistic entities, as the meaning-reference dichotomy implies, it
follows by symmetry that linguistic entities must also be in principle separable from extra-linguistic entities. In other words,
if there are pure 'referents,' unmixed with language, then there
are also pure 'meanings,' unmixed with experience. Thus the
meaning-reference dichotomy and the quest for 'referent'
gives rise to the analytic-synthetic distinction and the quest
for 'meaning'. For the problem of analyticity is ultimately
that of finding a criterion of meaning, and the analytic-synthetic distinction depends on such a criterion. The crucial test
of analyticity is identity of meaning. But a criterion of identity
presupposes that meanings are stable and fixed, and a ground
for such stability and fixity is provided by substance ontology.
To be sure, philosophers have differed on the question whether
meanings themselves had independent existence or 'subsistence'
but whether or not they do, the quest for identity demands an
objective criterion of meaning which may be found either in the
intrinsic nature of meanings themselves or in sense-experience
and, no matter which, in the last analysis, in substance ontology.

The Buddhist logicians' views on the problem of analyticity differ radically from all the above-mentioned and kindred
approaches. The Buddhists, first of all, do not recognize any
fundamental distinction between 'meaning' and 'reference.'
Hence they deny that identity of meanings is the ultimate criterion of analyticity, because 'meaning' itself, and even more so
'identity of meaning,' is, according to them, in need of clarifi-

cation and explanation. The Buddhist rejection of substance ontology, however, renders all attempts to posit an 'objective ground' of meanings either in the realm of meanings themselves or in the world of things inadmissible. It is no coincidence that such contemporary Western philosophers as W.V. Quine, who question the tenability of the analytic-synthetic distinction, are also critical of substance ontology. Quine, like the Buddhists, has come to the conclusion that there is a close connection between substance ontology which lurks behind most of the theories of meaning and reference and the belief that a sharp line can be drawn between the analytic and the synthetic.

The Buddhist logicians' approach to the problem of analyticity stems from their theory of reality, in particular, the view that language is incapable of representing reality and hence that conceptual knowledge is not 'about the world' in the sense in which it is commonly believed to be in the West. However, the Buddhists by no means wish to deny either reality or the existence of conceptual-empirical knowledge. Far from launching upon the grandiose task of either proving or disproving that the world is real, the main concern of the Buddhist logicians is simply to show why reality is not amenable to discourse and conceptualization. Naturally, having shown that nothing can be said about reality and, by implication, whatever can be said does not correspond to reality, the Buddhists must provide an explanation as to how men come to have conceptual-empirical knowledge at all and what kind of 'reality' is the object of such knowledge. (Of course the need for such an explanation does not arise if knowledge is believed to be firmly rooted in reality.) That is, having rejected the ontological basis for both fixity of reference and objectivity of meaning, the Buddhists must explain how concepts have meaning at all and what it is that they describe. This the Buddhists do by means of a theory of meaning known as apohavāda or bheda-grahavāda.

An exposition and critical examination of the Buddhist theories of reality and meaning are therefore a necessary preliminary to the main task of this book, which consists of comparing and contrasting the Buddhist logicians' views on meaning, reference, and analyticity with some of the most influential contemporary Western views on these issues. Accordingly, the next chapter will be concerned with the Buddhist theory of reality and contemporary Western approaches to problems of ontology.   In the next two chapters, a detailed examination of the meaning-reference dichotomy as formulated and inter-preted by Russell and Quine will be undertaken, followed by a discussion of the Buddhist theory of meaning and a critical examination of the meaning-reference dichotomy in the light of this theory.   The last two chapters will be concerned with the analytic-synthetic distinction, in which Quine's formulation and critique of the problem of analyticity will be discussed in detail and compared with the Buddhist approach to the analytic-synthetic distinction.

II

BUDDHIST THEORY OF REALITY AND SOME WESTERN VIEWS ON ONTOLOGY

The view which is commonly and correctly associated with Buddhism is that "in reality everything is in flux and nothing stays the same." But this phrase is sufficiently broad and vague to also correctly characterize views which are rejected by Buddhism. Thus a Buddhist would hasten to add that besides the flux and change there is nothing that undergoes flux and change—a point which is seldom emphasized even by the process-philosophers of the West. According to the Buddhists, change itself is reality and the moment of change which has no duration in time and no extension in space is the ultimate point of reality. The Buddhist logicians defend this theory of reality by means of a device called 'analytical deduction.' An analytical deduction consists of an inference on the basis of the sameness of referent of two different words.[1] But actually such a 'deduction' involves much more than is usually understood by the term. It involves penetrating analyses of linguistic phrases and expressions which purport to describe reality, showing that the ideas of laymen as well as of philosophers concerning the nature of reality are largely due to the influence of words and the grammatical structure of language; in particular, that the various theories concerning the nature of reality can be shown to arise from the belief that words which have distinct meanings also have distinct entities as their referents. Whereas,

> A mere idea, or a mere name, is a name to which nothing separate corresponds, which has no corresponding reality of its own. A pseudo-idea is a word to which nothing at all corresponds, as, e.g., "a flower in the sky."[2]

1. Th. Stcherbatsky, *Buddhist Logic*, Vol. I, Dover Publications, Inc., N. Y., 1962, pp. 90-91.
2. *Ibid.*, p. 92.

Examples of names to which nothing separate corresponds are 'existence' when it is thought to be something over and above the things that exist, and 'thing' when it is thought to be something over and above the qualities which it has.

It is both instructive and interesting to note that the point of the analytical deductions is thus exactly the same which has been made by Quine, namely, that ontology becomes unnecessarily populated due to hypostatization of linguistic entities. Quine shares, whether or not he is aware of it, the Buddhist logicians' conviction that ontological complexity only contributes to epistemological confusion and philosophical bewilderment. Much of Quine's logical and philosophical work is concerned with "cleaning up the ontological slums" which have flourished as a result of such hypostatizations. Thus there are certain striking similarities between Quine and the Buddhists both with respect to aim, namely, to expose the linguistic traps waiting to catch the theorist of reality, and with respect to the rigorous method of logical analysis in pursuit of this aim. But there are also subtle but important differences all of which are not rooted in conceptual disputes and hence cannot be settled by logical analysis alone. Some of them are matters of deeply ingrown attitudes, nurtured in long cultural tradition. Thus contemporary Western philosophers and logicians generally display aversion toward what are called 'genetic questions, that is, questions of origin or sources which threaten to lead to psychological considerations and metaphysical speculations. In this spirit, Karl Popper traces the causes of the sad state of contemporary epistemology to the ill-conceived questions of 'sources' :

> The traditional systems of epistemology may be said to result from yes-answers and no-answers to questions about the sources of our knowledge. *They never challenge these questions, or dispute their legitimacy*; the questions are taken as perfectly natural, and nobody seems to see any harm in them.[1]

Those who talk about origins or sources of knowledge are frequently guilty of confusing two things which ought to be

1. Karl Popper, *Conjectures and Refutations*, Basic Books, N.Y., 1962, p. 25.

kept separate, namely, explanation and justification. 'Origin' may mean either explanation or justification but not necessarily both. Explanation always entails either causal or logical relations between the explanandum and the explanans, whereas justification is not necessarily dependent on such relations. The important point which is often missed is that explanation does not entail justification, nor does justification entail explanation. Directed against those who equate 'source' with 'justification,' Popper's criticism is well-taken. Unfortunately, however, the confusion between explanation and justification is just as common among those who agree with Popper's criticism as it is among those who come under its fire. It may very well be the same confusion that cautions the former against theorizing about the sources of knowledge that also inspires the latter to search for answers where none exist. But why should one shun away from explaining, just because the explanations turn out to be "not good enough" (whatever that means) for purposes of justification ? On the contrary, it would seem that wisdom consists in taking a bold look into whatever the search for explanation may reveal and in realizing that the psychological tendencies and motivations and the fanciful, perhaps even faulty, beliefs concerning the nature of reality which may lie at the origin of our knowledge neither justify nor nullify our knowledge.

However, by far the more prevalent view among contemporary Western philosophers seems to be that all problems of knowledge and reality can be solved by logico-conceptual means, and those that cannot need not be recognized as problems at all. Some, though, take the humbler position of acknowledging that there are indeed genuine questions of ontology which cannot be settled by means of logical analysis, but they prefer to leave such questions unsettled rather than look for other means of settling them. Quine seems inclined toward the latter position. Thus commenting on Hume's account of "our ideas of external objects", Quine calls Hume's theory an interesting psychological conjecture" but feels that "there is no need for us to share that conjecture."[1] Nor does he feel

---

1. W. V. Quine, "Identity, Ostension, and Hypostasis," *From a Logical Point of View*, Harper Torchbooks, N. Y., 1963, p. 66.

the need to replace Hume's conjecture with a more satisfactory theory. For him "The important point to observe is merely the *direct connection* between identity and the positing of processes or time-extended objects."[1] The crucial ontological question— incidentally, the one which Hume tried to answer—remains, what kind of 'direct connection' is it ?

The above question points to one of the toughest problems in the Quinean counterpart of an account of our ideas of external objects. The same problem, however, is avoided by the Buddhist logicians whose analysis of existential statements is otherwise very similar to Quine's. Thus both Quine and the Buddhists reject the fundamental tenet of substance ontology, namely, that existence is a function of things. Furthermore, both agree that all statements about things can be reduced to statements describing the properties of things. The question on which Quine and the Buddhists differ is, what is existence ultimately a function of ? For Quine, existence is a function of '*having* predicates (or properties),' while for the Buddhists existence is a function of the predicates (or properties) them- selves. Statements of the type 'the jug is blue' are analyzed by Indian logicians in general and Buddhist logicians in particular "as descriptions of the conditions under which the attribute.. may be said to 'occur in' a 'locus'. . . . "[2] Thus the basic form of all statements, analyzed in terms of 'occurrence in a locus' is expressed by the formula 'O (f, a),' which reads 'f occurs in a.'[3] The basic form of all statements according to Quine is '($\exists$x) Fx' which is interpreted as 'there is an x such that x has the property F.'[4] In the Buddhist formula both the locus and that which occurs in the locus, a and f respectively, are specified through descriptions, and no subject appears over and above such descriptions. The subject is reduced to its predicates

1. *Ibid.*, p. 67, (italics added).

2. A. C. Senape McDermott, *An Eleventh-Century Buddhist Logic of 'Exists,'* Humanities Press, N. Y., 1970, p. 8.

3. *Ibid.*, Cf. B. M. Matilal's interpretation of qualificative cognition in the Nyāya as 'Q(...)' in his *The Navya-Nyāya Doctrine of Negation*, Harvard University Press, Cambridge, Mass., 1968, pp. 14-15. It should be emphasi- zed, however, that the term 'locus' signifies a substratum for the Nyāya Realists. whereas for the Buddhists it has no such significance.

4. W. V. Quine, *Word and Object*, The N. I. T. Press, 1965, pp. 162-3 176-80.

and in the last analysis every predicative judgment breaks down into a series of descriptions. Thus for the Buddhists, descriptions are the ultimate simples of logical analysis; there are no 'logical subjects' and hence no ontological bearers of descriptions. On the other hand, it is clear that in ' $(\exists x)$ Fx' 'x' is not a description but rather the bearer of descriptions. Insofar as for Quine, existence is a function of *having* predicates and x is that which has predicates, the problem of existence for Quine becomes the problem of determining what kind of entity x is.

Now it is a central point of Quine's critique of substance ontologies and one on which his own rejection of 'thing' or 'object' as an ontological category rests that 'x' has no intrinsic meaning or descriptive content. Rather, 'x' is considered a mere variable which acquires meaning solely by being connected to descriptive terms like 'F'. But what is the nature of the connection between 'x' and 'F'? It would seem that the connection must be identity, insofar as the meaning of 'x' is exhausted by 'F.' However, Quine is strongly opposed to interpreting the connection as being one of identity,[1] and the reason is obvious: 'F' and 'x' belong to the distinct categories of meaning and reference respectively, and to put an identity-sign between the two is to blur the distinction between these categories. But, more importantly, putting an identity-sign between 'F' and 'x' commits one to assign the same ontological status to them, and for such an avowed anti-Platonist as Quine, this would be plainly inconceivable. But the other alternative which Quine chooses, namely, that 'x' is not to be identified with its predicates, is beset with no less difficulties. For if 'x' and 'F' are not identical, then their difference must consist in some *intrinsic property* of 'x' which is not exhausted by 'F' and such other descriptions. Moreover, it must be this property which also warrants putting the existential quantifier before 'x.' What this property is, and more generally, what constitutes 'existence' as applied to things, events, processes, or anything at all, Quine never tells us. Instead, he reverts to behavioristic explanations of the type that when such-and-such conditions (specifying socially conformed verbal behavior) are fulfilled, people may be observed as a rule to use existentially quantified

1. W. V. Quine, *Word and Object*. p. 179

statements.[1] Such an account of our fundamental ontological commitments amounts to saying no more and no less than that people can be observed to employ the existential quantifier when they do. Quine may be right in concluding that "the question what ontology actually to adopt still stands open, and the obvious counsel is tolerance and experimental spirit;"[2] for that question is concerned with selecting the best or most correct ontology; in other words, it is concerned with justification. And for all we know, that question may remain open forever. Hence a liberal and permissive attitude toward problems of ontological justification may be in order, but that is not to say that one should not attempt a thorough and adequate explanation of at least those ontological beliefs and presuppositions, whether good, bad, well or ill-conceived, which must necessarily be accepted by anyone who engages in conceptual thinking.

The Buddhist logicians share none of the inhibitions from which Quine and other Western logicians suffer concerning the treatment of ontological issues. For one thing, in the Buddhist and in general Eastern view, the boundaries which divide knowledge into separate compartments or disciplines are neither very sharp nor irrevocable. Such boundaries merely serve the pragmatic purpose of facilitating inquiry and hence remain subservient to the goal of furthering and extending knowledge in all directions. Thus where inquiry demands moving from logic to epistemology or from epistemology to ontology and psychology, there the boundaries may be crossed. But a more important reason for the bold approach to ontological issues by the Buddhists is the fact that, unlike most of his Western colleagues who at the end of their inquiry may or may not give up the hope for ontological justification, the Buddhist starts with the conviction that his ontological inquiries will produce no justification for any system of knowledge or belief, and his interest in ontological issues grows mainly out of his desire to demonstrate the truth of this conviction. Thus for the Buddhist logician it is not enough to show that *so far* our efforts to find a 'true' ontology have failed and to conclude therefrom that they most likely will never succeed, as Quine does. The Buddhists con-

1. Quine, *Word and Object*, p. 17.
2. Quine, "On What There Is", *From a Logical Point of View*, p. 19.

tend that as long as there is even a shred of hope of finding a true ontology, there will always be people who waste their time and effort in search for one. Therefore, the Buddhists conclude, it will be to the best interest of everybody to put to final rest all such vain hopes. Apart from the therapeutic value which the Buddhist attitude may have, it has produced thorough and excruciating analyses of such notions as 'reality,' 'knowledge,' and 'existence.' Their purpose is to show that the lack of success in finding ontological justification for our beliefs and theories about the world is not due to the inadequacies or incompleteness of knowledge which one may hope to progressively eliminate, but to the very nature of thought.

However, a demonstration of the necessary failure of all attempts to find ontological justification of theories of reality appears, at least in the face of it, impossible. For such a demonstration seems to depend in part on the possibility of knowing what non-conceptual reality is like. But since knowledge (vijñāna) is conceptual, it follows that reality which is non-conceptual cannot be known and hence the demonstration is impossible. On the other hand, if reality could be known and the demonstration thus were possible, it would be self-contradictory. Thus, no matter which horn of the dilemma one chooses the demonstration seems doomed to failure.

One way in which the Buddhists may seek to escape the dilemma is to maintain that not all knowledge is conceptual and that besides conceptual knowledge (vijñāna) there is another, radically different kind of knowledge which is non-conceptual (parāvidyā). Thus while the immediate object of vijñāna is an image or conceptual construction which it takes to be reality, parāvidyā is the immediate, non-conceptual awareness of reality. The Buddhists hold that all men are in principle capable of both kinds of knowledge. To be sure, conceptual knowledge and experience mediated through conceptual constructions is the way of ordinary men, including the scientist, whereas the direct, non-conceptual awareness which alone is capable of reaching ultimate reality is a rare and extraordinary ability, possessed only by very few as a result of long and arduous practice. The ability in question is the yogic intuition (yogipratyakṣa). According to Dharmakīrti, "The (mystic) intuition of the Saint (the Yogī) is produced from the

subculminal state of deep meditation on transcendental reality."[1]
Since ultimate reality is knowable through yogipratyakṣa,
the doctrine of double-standard of reality is not a mere *ad hoc*
postulation for the purpose of supporting the theory that ultimate reality is necessarily beyond the reach of conceptual knowledge and provides no ontological ustification for any system
of knowledge.

However, the demonstration of the truth of the above
claim is not yet cleared of all difficulties. Granted non-conceptual knowledge of ultimate reality, such knowledge does
not seem to be of much help in a demonstration which employs
conceptual means—especially since Dharmakīrti explicitly denies
that there are non-conceptual judgments (nirvikalpaka) and
"refuses to call anything a judgment unless it is *savikalpaka*."[2]
If the object of the demonstration is the impossibility of conceptualizing about reality but the very showing of this necessitates
conceptualizing about it, it seems that the whole demonstration becomes an exercise in shadow-boxing. A Buddhist,
however, would be neither dismayed nor disheartened by such
dim prospects. On the contrary, he would be the first to point
out that conceptualization is indeed very much like shadow-
boxing—in particular the attempt to capture reality by conceptual means. He would therefore welcome the analogy as
conveying both epistemological and ontological insight. Thus
one stops chasing after shadows upon the realization that the
shadows are not objects outside oneself but merely reflections
of one's own movements. And the success of one's efforts
does not depend on one's actually catching anything but on
controlling one's movements or rather, ceasing to move altogether. So it is with conceptual knowledge and reality: one
stops looking for reality in images and conceptual constructions
upon the realization that the latter are merely projections from
one's own imagination. Thus, the more elaborate conceptual
systems and constructions one builds, the farther removed one
is from reality; and conversely, the simpler and fewer such

1. Dharmakīrti, *A Short Treatise of Logic (Nyāya-Bindu)* with *A Commentary (Ṭīkā)* by Dharmottara, *(Buddhist Logic*, Vol. II), tr. Th. Stcherbatsky,
Dover Publications, Inc., N. Y., 1962, p. 30. Hereafter referred to as *N.B.*
and *N.B.T.* respectively.
2. Karl Potter, *Presuppositions of India's Philosophies*, Prentice-Hall,
N. J., 1963, p. 197.

systems and constructions, the fewer the barriers which obstruct one's direct awareness of reality. As to reality itself, it cannot be identified with any of the images and constructions which constitute the immediate objects of conceptual knowledge anymore than it can be identified with the shadows on the walls which are the immediate objects of the boxer's attention. (The apparent similarity to Plato's cave notwithstanding, the author wishes to emphasize that the Buddhist logician does not fall victim to the Platonic lure that reality is to be grasped by a flight into the realm of forms, ideas, and essences.) This is to say that, from the conceptual point of view, ultimate reality vanishes to an extensionless point, incapable of either qualitative or quantitative determination.

The Buddhist logicians, it may be recalled, part company with Quine on what at first appeared an insignificant grammatical dispute over the proper place of the notion of 'existence' in existential statements. While Quine regards *existence as equivalent to having predicates*—a view which led to difficulties concerning the subject of the predicates—the Buddhists maintain that *existence is nothing over and above the predicates themselves.* Thus for the Buddhists the notion of 'existence' is inseparable from that of 'predicate' or 'quality'; there are no things that possess qualities or that are subjects of predicates but the qualities are all that there is. This means that there is no substratum underlying and unifying different qualities into predicates of one and the same thing. It follows that the concept of 'thing' becomes superfluous and useless, for to say that there are distinct things is equivalent to saying that there are distinct qualities. But to say either is equivalent to saying that there are distinct existences. In view of the Buddhist conception of reality as a process or a flux in which nothing stays the same, it follows that the ultimately distinct existence is a point-instant (svalakṣaṇa) which has neither duration in time nor extension in space. The notion of 'continuity' of 'extension' thus cannot be deduced from the reality of the point-instants; it presupposes entities which have spatial and temporal extension and hence it is a construction by the human mind. (It may be noted that this view of the Buddhists is in sharp contrast with Bergson's, according to which continuity as 'duration' is a directly experienced fundamental characteristic of reality.)

According to the Buddhists, therefore, space and time which presuppose extension and continuity are ideal constructions.[1]

Since reality is characterized by distinctness, the words 'existence' and 'non-existence' are equally applicable to it. This is not to say, however, that the Buddhists subscribe to the view which regards existence and non-existence as two distinct principles of reality. In such a view 'existence' implies endurance of some sort which when negated or annihilated becomes 'non-existence.' But 'endurance' is nothing but 'continuity' and thus a mere construction; whereas reality "cannot be divided into parts so that non-existence should follow upon existence: its evanescence arises simultaneously with its production, otherwise evanescence would not belong to the very essence of reality.[2] 'Existence' and 'non-existence' are thus not two distinct principles of reality but just different names given to the same reality—the reality of the point-instant. By means of a similar analysis it can be shown that causality, which is usually thought to be a relationship among existents, is nothing over and above these existents and that there are no other causes of things, or effects of things, than the things themselves. Thus 'cause' and 'thing', like 'existence' and 'non-existence' are not separate realities but names or characterizations of one and the same reality of the point-instant.

A few points of clarification concerning the notions of 'cause', 'thing,' and 'quality' may be in order here to ward off all suggestions that the Buddhist logicians subscribe to some sort of realist or correspondence theory of knowledge. To think that the Buddhists affirm the existence of either things, qualities, or causes would be to completely miss the point of the Buddhist analysis which is simply to show the interrelatedness and mutual dependence of the concepts of 'thing', 'quality', and 'cause' and not to affirm or deny the existence of anything. According to the Buddhists, these concepts do not denote independent realities, that is, they do not constitute distinct ontological categories. In other words, there are no qualities that are not things and no things that are not causes. However, this is not to be confused with a reduction of the three

---

1. Stcherbatsky, *Buddhist Logic*, Vol. I, p. 84.
2. *Ibid.*, p. 95.

categories to one, for example 'thing,' which would be to assign ontological status to things. The Buddhist point is, rather, that all three categories are only different ways of describing one and the same reality, and one could just as well say that there are no causes that are not things and no things that are not qualities.

However, the Buddhist view that ultimate reality is causally efficacious does imply that conceptual-empirical knowledge and the various conceptions of reality are causally related to the point-instants. The Buddhists readily admit this, but they would warn against confusing 'causal relations' with 'cognitive relations.' To maintain that the relationship between the point-instants of ultimate reality and the objects of conceptual-empirical knowledge is cognitive, i.e., logical or a priori, commits one to a correspondence theory of knowledge, whereas the view that the relationship is merely causal is quite compatible with the Buddhist contention that the point-instants are never objects of conceptual-empirical knowledge. The Vedantin example of the snake and the rope serves equally well to illustrate the Buddhist point. Thus one stumbles upon a rope in the dark and thinks it is a snake. The object of one's cognition at that moment is a snake, although the cause of the cognition is the rope. But to say that the object of cognition is the illusion of a snake is to confuse a predicate of the cognition with the cause of the cognition. Similarly, to think that 'things,' 'qualities' or 'causes' are the causes of the cognition of things, qualities, or causes is to mistake the predicates of cognition with the causes of cognition. Cognitive relations obtain amongst the predicates of cognition, whereas the predicates, including the relations, are causally related to the point-instants.

The foregoing analyses show that concepts like 'existence,' 'non-existence', 'thing', 'quality', and 'cause' which are thought to describe different things in reality or different aspects of reality actually have no distinct referents. The distinctions which are believed to exist among 'objects' or "facts" of the world have no cognitive basis in ultimate reality but are constructed:

Therefore it is said, "as regards reality," i.e., the two
  facts are identical with reference to what is the ultimately real essence, . . . But the constructed objects,

those (conceptions) which have been superimposed (upon reality), are not the same (in the facts constituting) the reason and the consequence. . . The possibility of deducing the one fact from the other always reposes upon a necessary (connection between them). Therefore their difference (in an analytical deduction) concerns exclusively those (constructed) conceptions which have been superimposed (upon the same reality) and which are necessarily (connected). The (underlying) reality is the same.[1]

As far as ultimate reality is concerned, the complexity and diversity of an ontology projected by such constructions reduces to the monotony and simplicity of the point-instant. The point of the Buddhist analytical deductions therefore is that all speculative attempts to capture ultimate reality are futile. Nothing can be said about a point-instant, except to give it a name, and one name is as illuminating or obscure as another.

The implicit message of the Buddhist theory of reality seems to be that contemplation is preferable to conceptualization, silence to talk, as means of knowing what there really is; and such an approach is certainly not discouraged by the Buddhists. Nonetheless, for the benefit of those who still wish to pursue the way of discourse and conceptual knowledge, it must be emphasized that the real significance of the point-instant theory lies not in its being an ontological claim but in its being an epistemological claim about conceptual thought and knowledge, namely, that the nature of language and conceptual thought is such that these necessarily fall short of capturing the point-instant. This gives the clue as to how the Buddhists will proceed to demonstrate their claim. The demonstration will consist in determining what are the necessary conditions of all conceptual thought, irrespective of what beliefs and presuppositions may be associated with different systems of thought and knowledge, and in showing that the necessary conditions involve a negation of reality.

Since negation of reality is illusion, the Buddhist thesis

1. Dharmakīrti, *N.B.*, pp. 73-74.

amounts to no less than the claim that, from the standpoint of ultimate reality, all knowledge is illusory.   Thus, while Popper in protesting against the futile search for the 'sources' of knowledge did not answer as to why such a search is futile,[1] the Buddhists give an answer which is meant to be not just discouraging but disillusioning in the most ruthlessly literal sense of the term: according to the Buddhists, the source of conceptual thought and knowledge is illusion and ignorance. The ignorance which thus gives rise to all knowledge consists in the failure to see the ultimate differences of things (i.e., the point-instants).[2] It is not that upon discoursing about the world, people sometimes ignore differences and unique characteristics of things but that they *necessarily* do so whenever they engage in conceptual thought and discourse. This is because the perception of similarities is a necessary condition for the possibility of conceptualization and discourse, whereas, according to the Buddhists, in the point-instant reality there is nothing similar but everything is absolutely dissimilar with everything else. Thus, the perception of similarities where none exist is illusion, and the non-perception of the differences is ignorance. And it is this illusion which on the one hand keeps man ignorant of ultimate reality and on the other hand makes conceptualization, language, and therewith knowledge possible.

However, it seems that if 'similarity' is a necessary condition for conceptualization, so is 'difference,' since the two are polar concepts. Are the Buddhists then to be understood as rejecting one of the polar concepts, 'similarity,' while preserving the other, 'dissimilarity' or 'difference'? If this were indeed what the Buddhists mean, nothing could save them from the disastrous consequences entailed by it. For if the meaning of 'absolutely dissimilar,' as applied to the point-instant, were understood as the opposite of 'similar' then it would be dependent on and produced by the meaning of 'similar,' just as the meaning of 'similar' is dependent on and produced by that of 'different. But then how can one be said to be real and the other illusion? If similarities are illusory, then certainly differences must be equally illusory. From this it follows that every-

1.   Popper, *Conjectures and Refutations*, pp. 25-27.

2.   Potter, *Presuppositions of India's Philosophies*, p. 188.

thing, including the reality of the point-instant, is illusion. But then the meaning of 'illusion' becomes vacuous since it cannot be contrasted with anything which is not illusory.

The Buddhists, however, do not mean by 'absolutely dissimilar' anything that is understood by means of a contrast with 'similar', and the real meaning of the dictum that "only the absolutely dissimilar is real, whereas the similar is illusion" is not that one of the poles in the similar-different polarity is illusion but that *the polarity itself* and therewith all discourse and discursive knowledge are illusion. The rejection of the category of 'similarity' makes discourse impossible; but so would, for that matter, the rejection of the category of 'difference.' In fact the rejection of one implies the rejection of the other. For all polar terms, such as 'tall' and 'short,' 'broad' and 'narrow,' acquire their meanings by being contrasted with each other. They are thus mutually dependent and each becomes meaningless if deprived of the other pole. 'Similarity' and 'difference' are in this sense polar terms. Moreover. 'similarity' and 'difference' are the two categories which underlie all other polarities and form the necessary condition for the possibility of conceptualization. Hence the rejection of one of them is sufficient to make all discourse impossible. To illustrate the point, assume that there are no similarities in the world. There would then be no criterion by which individual things can be grouped together under one name and singled out from the rest of the world. Contrariwise, one may assume that there are no differences in the world but everything is similar in all respects with everything else. In such a situation it would be impossible to say of any group of things that they are similar, let alone that they are different, since there is in the first place no criterion for distinguishing one group of things from another. The matter may be put more pointedly as follows: If there are no similarities in the world but everything is wholly different from everything else, then a word which refers to something at one moment refers to nothing at all the next moment. If, on the other hand, there are no differences in the world but everything is similar to everything else, then a word which refers to one thing at one moment also refers to all other things at all times. In either case, meaningful discourse about the world is impossible.

The Buddhists are fully aware of the implication of their pronouncement that "similarity is illusion" namely, that discourse about reality is impossible. Therefore, the charge that the Buddhists reject one of the polar terms while keeping the other is not valid. For the dissimilarity of the point-instant reality transcends all polarities and all discourses. There is, however, a point which can be legitimately brought against the Buddhists: if 'dissimilarity' as applied to the point-instants transcends the similar-different polarity, then why call the point-instants 'dissimilar'? From the point of view which transcends all polarities and all conceptual systems built upon such polarities, there is no difference between 'similar' and 'dissimilar'. This only shows that, even if it is true that "any name is as illuminating or obscure as another as far as ultimate reality is concerned," it is also true that even to give a name is already to say something about that which is named. Thus if the Buddhists were to abide by their conviction that nothing at all can be said about ultimate reality, they should refrain from even calling it by a name. However, it is to be noted that the fact that the Buddhists talk about 'point-instants' turns out illegitimate on their own premises does not constitute a proof of some basic fallacy in the Buddhist analysis of conceptual thought and knowledge. If anything, it is one more testimony to the predicament of language which no one who embarks upon discourse, even if for the purpose of destroying discourse, can escape.

III

MEANING, REFERENCE, AND ONTOLOGICAL COMMITMENTS IN RUSSELL AND QUINE

It is a truism that as long as one is in a state of illusion one does not know it, and conversely, as soon as one knows it, one is no longer in it. It is therefore not surprising that what for Aristotle was the most certain truth about the world, namely that "a thing is what it is and is not what it is not," is from the Buddhist point of view the supreme illusion. While most Western thinkers take issue with Aristotle's interpretation of the Law of Identity, in particular his belief that it expresses a truth about the world, few are prepared to say that Aristotle suffered from illusion.

To be sure, contemporary Western philosophers have gone a long way from the Platonic and Aristotelian world-views. The trend has been to relegate into the realm of meanings most of those entities which used to belong to the Platonic world of ideas or the Aristotelian world of things, and the new interpretation of the Law of Identity was rendered appropriately "a word means (or a proposition says) what it means and not what it does not." Thus the world was left bare and empty of the forms, essences, and universals which used to provide order and significance to it. With Russell and Quine, even the existence of particular things which used to constitute the bulk of the material world became threatened. Nevertheless one suspects that in spite of, or perhaps indeed because of, the logically sound but existentially barren world-view proclaimed by philosophers and logicians, the world in which men, including philosophers, actually live remained more or less as it had always been, which is more or less as Aristotle had described it. Thus the philosophers' strictures upon 'existence' only contributed to the widening of a gulf between the world-view proclaimed by philosophy and that of everyday experience, so that while on the one hand the sorts of things that could (philosophically) be *said* to exist became fewer and fewer until practically none were left, on the other hand the belief persisted that things as we experience them *do* exist, the philosopher notwithstanding. It is not surprising, then that a radically new approach which became known as "ordinary language philosophy" suddenly won converts among those who felt themselves caged in the barren philosophical mansions, cut off from the "real world of flesh and blood." The philosophers of "ordinary language" contend that philosophers only talk about words—and even about them confusedly most of the time—but they have nothing to say about the world in which men live and experience. According to this view, the way to learn about the world is by listening to the talk of ordinary men in the street rather than to the musings of philosophers in the ivory tower. However, insofar as there were some philosophers who still insisted that they have something to say about the world, the rift between the philosophical world-view and the beliefs and attitudes of everyday experience became a problem for philosophy itself. Much ontological status of universals by conferring upon them a quasi-ontological status which, for all practical purposes, is just as good as the original. This attempt has resulted in what Morton White calls 'duovocalism' and 'multivocalism.' Duovocalism is the theory that there are two kinds of existence, 'existence' and 'subsistence,' corresponding to the modes of being of non-conceptual things and conceptual meanings respectively. Multivocalism holds that there are as many different kinds of existence or senses of 'exist' as there are types or categories of entities. The doctrine of duovocalism was set forth by Bertrand Russell as follows :

> Thus thoughts and feelings, minds and physical objects *exist*. But universals do not exist in this sense : we shall say that they *subsist* or *have being*, where 'being' is opposed to 'existence' as being timeless. The world of universals, therefore, can also be described as the world of being. The world of being is unchangeable, rigid, exact, delightful to the mathematician, the logician, the builder of metaphysical systems, and all who love perfection more than life. The world of existence is fleeting, vague, without sharp boundaries, without any clear plan or arrangement, but it contains all thoughts and feelings, all the data of sense, and all physical objects, everything that

can do either good or harm, everything that makes
any difference to the value of life and the world.[1]

Multivocalism, on the other hand, follows from Gilbert
Ryle's famous theory of the different types or categories of
entities :

It is perfectly proper to say, in one logical tone of voice
that there exist minds and to say, in another logical
tone of voice, that there exist bodies. But these
expressions do not indicate two different species
of existence, for 'existence' is not a generic word like
'coloured' or 'sexed.' They indicate two different
senses of 'exist,' somewhat as 'rising' has different
senses in 'the tide is rising,' 'hopes are rising,' and
'the average age of death is rising.'[2]

Thus Russell and Ryle both seem assured that just about
anything can exist, somehow or other, in one sense or another.
However, such a generosity betrays a lack of worldly wisdom
which teaches that one can't both eat the cake and have it too.
For the suggestion seems to be that by merely changing from the
old way of talking about "existence of different substances"
to a new way of talking about "different kinds of senses of
existence" it is possible to both preserve the richness and eliminate the burden of traditional ontology. But without dwel-
ling further upon the merits and demerits of these and kindred
attempts to rescue the Platonic and Aristotelian world-views
from the disastrous attacks by the anti-Platonic and anti-Aristo-
telian critics, while at the same time trying to make these world-
views palatable to the critics, suffice it to quote Morton White
who aptly remarks,

Is it not strange, then, that e.g. Russell should say to the
ordinary man that he is proving the existence of
universals in another sense of 'exists'?....If a philosopher is going to be clever and prove that there are
more things than an ordinary man thinks there are,
he should not change the meaning of 'there are' in

1. Bertrand Russell, *The Problems of Philosophy*, A Galaxy Book, Oxford
University Press, N. Y., 1960, p. 100.
2. Gilbert Ryle, *The Concept of Mind*, Hutchinson's University Library,
London, 1949, p. 23.

the middle of the argument. Something similar is
clearly relevant in theology.[1]

The root of ontological anxiety is the feeling that there is
a world apart from one's knowing it; from such feeling arises the
concern with "things that exist" as distinct from "things that are
cognized." Ontological anxiety, therefore, lies at the basis of all
attempts to find a connection between the conceptual world of
meanings and the non-conceptual world of things. There are
two avenues to pursue the connection : one may try to locate the
points at which words make contact with things, in other words,
search for a criterion of 'reference'; or, one may try to establish
a basis for correlating descriptions with what they describe, in
other words, search for a criterion of 'meaning.' The two
approaches have their common origin in the assumption that a
clear-cut distinction can be established between 'meaning' and
'reference.'

The meaning-reference dichotomy in general and the
problem of finding a criterion of 'reference' in particular will
be dealt with next. The positions of Russell and Quine on
these issues will be examined in detail in the present chapter,
followed by a discussion of the Buddhist analysis of 'meaning'
and 'reference' in the next chapter. A comparison of the three
positions is both interesting and illuminating in that it reveals
vast differences of views concerning issues which are regarded
by many as self-evident and indisputable. Thus three distinct
positions will emerge from this comparison concerning the possibility of finding criteria of 'reference' and the viability of the
meaning-reference dichotomy: (1) the meaning-reference dichotomy is fundamental and beyond question, and it is possible to
find absolute (realistic) criteria of 'reference'; (2) the meaning-
reference dichotomy is fundamental and beyond question,
but it is possible to establish only relative and contextual (pragmatic) criteria of 'reference' and hence there are more than one
way of drawing the distinction between meaning and reference;
(3) neither the meaning-reference dichotomy nor any criteria
claimed for 'reference' are fundamental and beyond question,
and hence not only can the distinction between meaning and
reference be drawn in more than one way but it need not, and

1. Morton White, *Toward Reunion in Philosophy*, Atheneum, N.Y., 1963,
p. 77.

ultimately cannot, be drawn at all. The three positions correspond to Russell, Quine, and the Buddhist logicians respectively.

   To start with, some general observations will be made
concerning the meaning-reference dichotomy. The need for
a distinction between meaning and reference does not arise in
either of the two situations : when a complete isomorphism is
believed to exist between language and the world, in which
case a word which has a meaning also has a referent and vice
versa, meaning and reference thus being one and the same thing;
or when no correspondence whatsoever is thought to exist
between language and the world either through similarity of
logical structures or of words and objects, in which case it is
not possible to even talk about 'reference' in the commonly
understood sense of the term. The former characterizes the
Platonic and Aristotelian world-views, while the latter is the
final position of the Buddhist logicians. What gives rise to the
meaning-reference dichotomy is the position in the middle,
that is, the somewhat critical and cautious attitude toward
claims about the kinship between language and reality, which
yet does not amount to a total rejection of the belief in the basic
ability of language to depict reality. From the viewpoint of
the middle position, therefore, there is an obvious advantage in
drawing a distinction between meaning and reference. For it
enables one to maintain that not all words that have meaning
necessarily refer to anything in the world, thus making it easy
to dismiss the most extravagant claims of the Platonists while
preserving what seems modest and reasonable enough assumptions about the world. Thus the meaning-reference dichotomy
is not a mere linguistic conjecture for the logician's convenience,
as is sometimes thought. Rather, it is an ontological principle
which provides a gateway, however narrow, from words to
things. Moreover, as Quine came to suspect, it is a gateway
which, once it is opened even a little, can let back in the whole
of the Platonic or Aristotelian or any other world which a philosopher may wish to preserve and perpetuate. In the face of
a long tradition which has nourished theories about the existence
of such a gateway—among which Russell's theory of descriptions is the most recent and most influential—Quine's unorthodox
suspicions have led him to a curious position where he is not
prepared to deny that the gateway exists but only wants to keep

it firmly closed. More will be said about Quine's difficulties later in this chapter.

As it stands, the meaning-reference dichotomy is in need of clarification and revision on at least two accounts. First, the dichotomy itself must be sharpened and second, criteria must be provided for determining which words, if any, refer. According to Russell and Quine, every word (noun or adjective) belongs to one of the two mutually exclusive categories, namely, those that refer or in the terminology of Russell and Quine, 'denote,' and those that have meaning or 'describe.' Thus no descriptive terms refer to anything in the world, and conversely, no words that refer to the world have any descriptive content or meaning. This enables one to dispose of the last remnants of the grand Platonic world of essences. Not only that, most of those words that seem to refer to things actually turn out to be descriptions of them, and thus even the more modest Aristotelian world of things can be made to vanish. To show precisely this is the aim of both Russell and Quine. Thus Russell's theory of definite descriptions is designed to eliminate all 'denoting phrases,' that is to say, words and phrases that appear to refer rather than merely describe.[1] Quine's 'program of regimentation' whereby singular terms purporting to denote unique entities are regarded as general terms which do not denote anything follows closely the method provided by Russell's theory.[2]

Foregoing the details of the well-known theory of definite descriptions, the gist of the theory is as follows. All words and phrases, including proper names, which occur as subjects of sentences and purport to refer to unique extra-linguistic entities can by logical analysis be shown to be really predicates and hence as not referring but only describing. The uniqueness of reference of definite descriptions is taken care of by means of the three logical devices, existential quantifier, universal quantifier, and identity operator. Thus the existential quantifier '$(\exists x)$' guarantees that there is at least one entity to which a given set of descriptions belong, while the universal quantifier '(y)' to-

---

1. Bertrand Russell, "On Denoting," *Logic and Knowledge*, ed. R. C. Marsh, The Macmillan Co., Gt.B., 1964—pp. 41-56.
2. W. V. Quine, *Word and Object*, pp. 170-190.

gether with the identity operator ' = ' take care of the "at most"
requirement by stipulating that all those entities to which belongs the same set of descriptions are identical with x.   Thus
let 'P' and 'Q' stand for descriptions, then the logical form of all
descriptions of the type "the so-and-so is such-and-such" will be

$$(\exists x) \ [Px \ . \ Qx \ . \ (y) \ (Py \supset x=y) \ ].$$

The celebrated accomplishment of the theory of definite descriptions is that a unique reference can now be made without
directly identifying the object of reference with the general
terms that describe it.   Hence the use of general terms need not
commit one to an ontology of entities described by such terms.

Difficulties appear, however, when one moves from the
logical analysis of unique reference to the epistemological question as to what conditions must be fulfilled in order that the
kind of unique reference whose logical structure is depicted
above can be made. The epistemological question comes to
this : How is the bearer of the descriptions, i.e., the referent
of the subject term, identified in the first place so that descriptions can be predicated of it ?   Moreover, must it not be assumed
that there actually is something to be identified, before one
can seriously talk about ways and means of identifying referents ?
Thus the epistemological problem concerning the ways of knowing referents leads to the ontological problem as to what counts
as a 'referent.' Russell is prepared to face both problems,
which he considers central to any viable theory of knowledge.
Thus he regards it as at least a necessary condition for the possibility of empirical knowledge that the object whose description
is given be identifiable. A description or a denoting phrase
"is essentially *part* of a sentence, and does not, like most single
words, have any significance on its own account."[1] Therefore,
unless the description is associated with some definite, identifiable referent, the description cannot be understood simply
because there would be no way of knowing what it is a description of.[2] According to Russell, then, there are words which

1.   Russell, 'On Denoting," *Logic and Knowledge*, p. 51.

2. For this reason Russell calls descriptions 'incomplete symbols'
"which have absolutely no meaning whatsoever in isolation but merely acquire
meaning in a context," i.e., when they are connected to a subject which in
the last analysis is the logically proper name. ("The Philosophy of Logical
Atomism," *Logic and Knowledge*, p. 253.)

are purely referential, that is, they are genuine subjects whose referents are the bearers of descriptions. Such words are called by Russell 'logically proper names,' an example of which is the word 'this.' Thus all statements asserting something about the world are reducible in the last analysis to the form "this is that," where any description may be substituted for 'that' and 'this' is the subject of all such descriptions. The word 'this' has no meaning apart from the context in which it occurs as a subject of descriptions. Its meaning is its denotation, which is to say that its sole function in a statement is to refer.

The answer to the question as to how the referent of 'this' is known is provided by Russell's theory of knowledge. According to Russell, there are only two ways of obtaining knowledge about the world. These are : knowledge by acquaintance and knowledge by description. The former consists in direct sense-experience and is the basis of all other kinds of knowledge, including knowledge by description. The referent of 'this' then, is the object of direct sense-experience.[1] For Russell, the objects of direct sense-experience are 'sense-data.' At first sight the statement "the object of direct sense-experience is sense-data" seems to involve no ontological claim, insofar as 'sense-data' merely refers to the content of sense-experience. However, upon closer scrutiny it is evident that either an ontological claim is involved or the statement is vacuous and at bottom circular. It is vacuous and circular if 'sense-data' is taken to be just 'object of sense-experience' and nothing more and nothing less is meant by it. For if one asks, what kinds of things are 'objects of sense-experience'; the only answer is, 'sense-data.' But as soon as the object of experience is considered to be distinct from and something over and above the experiencing of the object, the question arises, what constitutes the object as distinct from the experience; and that, of course, is an ontological question. Even if nothing else can be said about the nature of sense-data, Russell (at least in the period of his 'Logical Atomism') would want to maintain that sense-data are 'ultimate particulars' which are not to be identified with the experiencing of the particulars.[2] This leads to the more general

1. Russell, "The Philosophy of Logical Atomism," *Logic and Knowledge*, p. 201.
2. *Ibid.*, p. 280.

thesis that there are extra-linguistic 'facts' about which asser-
tions are made in linguistic phrases.   In Russell's words

> In speaking of these facts, I am not alluding to the phrases
> in which we assert them, or to our frame of mind
> while we make the assertions, but to those features
> in the constitution of the world which make our
> assertions true (if they are true) or false (if they are
> false).[1]

But just that much is enough to commit him to the existence of
something besides the mere having of experiences. According
to Russell, the bridge from language to the world is a "revoca-
ble, temporary a priori connection" which holds between the
ultimate linguistic particular, the logically proper name, and
the ultimate extra-linguistic particular, sense-data.

Much as Quine admires Russell's theory of descriptions,
he cannot bring himself to accept Russell's theory of knowledge
which the latter considered to be intimately connected with the
theory of descriptions.   For Quine, the most enlightening and
intellectually liberating discovery of the theory of descriptions
is that one can talk meaningfully about what the world is *like*
without the need to speculate *what* it is.   This accords with his
conviction that besides descriptions (which tell us what the world
is like) there is strictly nothing else that can be conveyed about
the world by means of words.   Talk about 'extra-linguistic
particulars' and the connection between these and linguistic
particulars is, according to Quine, metaphysical speculation
which can neither be vindicated nor disproven by what can
actually be known.   Quine therefore wants to show that the
theory of descriptions need not entail Russell's theory of knowledge or, for that matter, any other theory about the connection
between language and the world.   According to Quine, there
is no reason to give the privileged status of referential words to
the one species of names which Russell calls 'logically proper
names,' but all names, including the logically proper names,
can be, and should be, eliminated.   If this means that for Quine,
no ontological commitments whatsoever are necessary, much
less desirable, in order that one may discourse about the world

---

1. Russell, "On Propositions : What they Are and How They Mean,"
Logic and Knowledge, p. 285.

in the manner prescribed by the theory of descriptions, then one would expect the next step for Quine to be the rejection of the meaning-reference dichotomy. For the meaning-reference dichotomy seems to be inextricably bound up with ontological commitments. Thus it is not only entailed by any and all assumptions and theories concerning the relationship between language and the world (except for the theory of complete isomorphism), but it also entails some such assumption or theory. However, Quine is not prepared to reject the meaning-reference dichotomy as basic to all statements which assert something about the world. Accordingly, he adopts Russell's analysis of such statements into the basic form '$(\exists x)\ Fx$' without qualification or modification. Moreover, he agrees with Russell that one is committed to the referent of the subject term for which the bound variable 'x' stands in the formula : "A theory is committed to those and only those entities to which the bound variables of the theory must be capable of referring in order that the affirmations made in the theory be true."[1]

Therefore, the dispensability of all ontological commitments is clearly not what Quine means when he denies that names have any special claims to referential position. What he means is that the theory of descriptions does not tell us what the referent of the bound variable is, and certainly it does not tell us that it is sense-data, as Russell believes. Rather,

> We look to bound variables in connection with ontology not in order to know what there is, but in order to know what a given remark or doctrine, ours or someone else's, says there is; and this much is quite properly a problem involving language. But what there is is another question.[2]

It is not the case that Quine denies the legitimacy of the latter question, either. Quite the contrary, he generously grants that there may be indefinitely, if not infinitely, many ways of answering the ontological question concerning what there is, and one answer could be sense-data. What Quine does deny is the claim that one answer is correct to the exclusion of others. This is the crux of his ontological relativism. According to Quine, our

1. Quine, "On What There Is," *From a Logical Point of View*, pp. 13-14.
2. *Ibid.*, p. 16.

choice of ontological alternatives must not be dictated by considerations of correctness or incorrectness : "It is meaningless...
to inquire into the absolute correctness of a conceptual scheme
as a mirror of reality.   Our standard for appraising basic changes
of conceptual scheme must be, not a realistic standard of correspondence to reality, but a pragmatic standard."[1]   The pragmatic standard depends on the purpose at hand in a given context of discourse.

    However, since purposes are in part at least dependent on
and defined by the context in which they are conceived and the
context in turn contains at least some ontological assumptions,
Quine's appeal to a pragmatic standard begs the question.
If question-begging and circularity are to be avoided, the referential or identificatory function of the bound variable must be
explained without appeal either to purposes or pragmatic considerations with respect to such purposes.   Strawson in an attempt
to interpret and throw light on Quine's position offers the following definition of the identificatory function of the bound variable:

> That function is successfully performed if and only if the
> singular term used establishes for the hearer an iden-
> tity, and the right identity, between the thought of
> *what-is-being-spoken-of-by-the-speaker* and the thought
> of some object *already within the reach of the hearer's
> own knowledge, experience, or perception*, some object,
> that is, which the hearer could, in one way or other,
> pick out or identify for himself, from his own resources.[2]

But what constitutes "resources of knowledge" and what enables
the hearer to correctly identify the object of the speaker's
thought ? The above definition does not seem to escape the
circularity, insofar as the answer to these questions is given by
appeal to the identificatory function of the bound variable which
is precisely what needs to be explained.   An alternative (which
Quine rejects) considered by Strawson is to "supply the hearer
with resources of knowledge which constitute, so to speak, a

    1. Quine, "Identity, Ostension, and Hypostasis," *From a Logical
Point of View*, p. 79.

    2. P. F. Strawson, "Singular Terms and Predication," *Words and
Objections, Essays on the Work of W. V. Quine*, D. Davidson & J. Hintikka, eds.,
Synthese Library, D. Reidel Publishing Co., Dordrecht-Holland, (Humani-
ties Press), pp. 106.

minimal basis for subsequent identifying reference to draw on."[1] This is what Russell does. The act of supplying resources in his case consists in simply saying that the referent is sense-data, and his explanation of the identificatory function of the bound variable consists in saying what the bound variable identifies, i.e., refers to. But Quine refuses to say that the bound variable identifies sense-data or anything else. This is not to say, however, that he denies that the bound variable has an identificatory function. He does deny that the bound variable supplies new resources.[2] And in so doing he is left without explanation, save a circular one, as to how any resources, new or old (which at one time were also new) come to be supplied in the first place.

Besides the charge of circularity, Quine also faces the following difficulty as to which names should occupy referential position in a sentence. Prima facie there is nothing in the formula '(x) Fx' to suggest which terms, if any, should occupy the referential position. Thus the bound variable might stand for an abstract singular term which is manufactured out of a descriptive general term, like 'beauty' out of 'beautiful.' Insofar as the formula lends itself to such interpretations, it is no more and no less reliable guide to drawing the distinction between terms that refer and those that do not than the grammar of ordinary language is. Yet according to Quine, "the division the words that are to be viewed as referring to objects of some sort, and the words that are not, is not to be drawn on grammatical lines."[3] Moreover, people often talk about things like 'beauty', 'honesty', etc. without necessarily believing that such *things* exist. This means that Quine is not correct in maintaining even that we can determine what somebody *says* there is by merely looking at the quantified variable—unless there is some hitherto unmentioned rule which says that one must not quantify over abstract singular terms and consequently also a criterion for determining what kinds of terms can be quantified. Since such criterion would specify which terms qualify to refer, the existence of such criterion would also provide a non-circular answer as to what constitutes an ontological commitment.

1. P. F. Strawson, "Singular Terms and Predication," *Words and Objections, Essays on the Work of W. V. Quine*, D. Davidson & J. Hintikka, eds., Synthese Library, D. Reidel Publishing Co., Dordrecht-Holland, (Humanities Press), pp. 106-107.
2. *Ibid.*, p. 107.   3. Quine, *Word and Object*, p. 16.

Quine's method for eliminating terms from referential positions provides explicit criteria for determining which terms do *not* qualify to refer, i.e., all those terms to which the method of elimination is applicable. But does Quine have a criterion for determining which terms do qualify to refer ? That '(ꓱx) Fx' rather than some other formula expresses the basic form of all existential statements means that in any given context of discourse, when all terms that can be eliminated have been eliminated, there will remain some which cannot be eliminated but must be considered as genuinely referring. To be sure, Quine is not very helpful on this point but leaves it for others, such as Strawson, to make explicit the criterion which he employs implicitly for determining which terms should refer. According to Strawson, the criterion is that of 'lower' and 'higher' types to which referential and predicative terms respectively belong :

> Two terms coupled in a true sentence stand in referential and predicative positions, respectively, if what the first term designates or signifies is a case or instance of what the second term signifies. Items thus related (or the terms that designate or signify them) may be said respectively to be of lower and higher type; and this is why I called the new criterion one of type.[1]

Thus the identificatory function of referential terms is to be explained in terms of the type-criterion. But if by 'particular' or 'lower type' were meant just that which is supposedly identified by the referential term, Strawson's proposal would be of little help in solving the problem of circularity. If circularity is to be avoided, what counts as a particular must be determined without appeal to the referential function of a term. According to Strawson, the independent criterion of a particular is 'spatio-temporality,' and the distinction between spatio-temporal particulars on the one hand and property-like principles of grouping such particulars on the other is the principle upon which the distinction between referential and predicative terms is based.[2]

Assuming that Strawson's interpretation of Quine is

---

1.   Strawson, "Singular Terms and Predication," *Words and Objections,* p. 111.

2.   *Ibid.,* pp. 114-115.

correct, one might ask, is the answer given by Strawson in principle different from that given by Russell? It seems that to say "the referent of the bound variable is a spatio-temporal particular" supplies the hearer with resources of knowledge just as much as to say that the referent is sense-data does. And whether commitment to spatio-temporal particulars is more sensible or otherwise advantageous than commitment to sense-data is a matter of individual taste and preference. The point is that even if Quine does not accept Strawson's interpretation and the commitment to spatio-temporal particulars, he will have to accept some other but equivalent interpretation if he is to give a non-circular explanation of the distinction between referential and predicative terms. Thus the semantical formula "to be is to be a value of a variable" does not, contrary to Quine's claim, merely serve "in testing the conformity of a given remark or doctrine to a prior ontological standard,"[1] but it also legislates that such a prior ontological standard must exist.

Although Quine's concession to ontology does not amount to very much, it is nevertheless more than what he originally intended. That is to say, if what Quine intended to say concerning the relationship between language and the world was that language can take one no farther in grasping the world than descriptions can. The conclusion to be drawn from the latter assertion would seem to be that since descriptions need not commit one to the existence of anything, language can at last be liberated from the age-old ontological burden. However, Quine's acceptance of the formula '$(\exists x)\ Fx$' repudiates such a conclusion, for it shows that it is not the descriptions that try to reach out into the world but the quantified variable. And *how* it reaches and how far it gets, Quine leaves for Russell, Strawson, and others to tell.

The difference between Russell and Quine with respect to their ontological commitments may now be summarized. For this purpose, a distinction will be introduced between first-order ontological statements and second-order ontological statements, hereafter denoted by S and S' respectively. Thus S is a statement of the type "s exists and is the referent of 'x' in '$(\exists x)$

---

1. Quine, "On What There Is," From a Logical Point of View, p. 15.

Fx,' " where s stands for sense-data or spatio-temporal object or some other entity. S′ is a statement of the type "x exists and is the referent of 'x' in '(ꟼx)Fx,' " where x stands for unspecified something. There may be several S statements corresponding to the different interpretations of 's,' but there can be only one S′ statement as no interpretation is given to 'x.' It is easy to see that generally S entails S′; but it is not clear in what sense, if any, S′ entails S. Thus while all and any S statements entail S′ it is obviously not correct to say that S′ entails all and any S statements. Nevertheless, it seems that S′ must entail at least some S statement. Otherwise, as was seen in the foregoing, the explanation of the distinction between the roles of referential and predicative terms in sentences remains circular, and as a consequence, there would be no criterion for distinguishing between meaning and reference at all. Thus, although acceptance of S′ does not compel one to accept any particular S statement, it compels one to accept *some S or other.*

Since all first-order ontological statements of the type S are mutually incompatible, i.e., one cannot subscribe to the ontology of, e.g., sense-data and physical objects at the same time, it follows that acceptance of any S statement commits one to ontological absolutism. Insofar as Russell subscribes to sense-data, he is in this sense an ontological absolutist. Acceptance of S′, on the other hand, commits one to ontological relativism, insofar as one is not thereby committed exclusively to any particular S statement. Quine is in this sense an ontological relativist, granting, of course, the equal plausibility of other interpretations besides Strawson's. But it is now clear what 'ontological relativism' of the Quinean variety means. It is often thought, not the least by Quine himself, that it means a 'neutral' position from which one can impartially describe the various ontological commitments that people make. However, fruitful and illuminating as such descriptions may otherwise be, they do not constitute an argument for genuine ontological relativism, any more than pointing to the existence of the various religious systems establishes that they are all equally true or false. The air of detachment which one may assume in describing the different ontological doctrines and beliefs is not to be mistaken for a demonstration that one does not, or need not, subscribe to any such doctrines and beliefs oneself. Contrary to common belief which may be due to such a mistake, Quine's ontological relativism is not free from ontological commitments. Even if the second-order ontological statement S′ to which Quine is minimally committed is not regarded as a genuine ontological commitment in itself, it eventually compels him to face a choice among the first-order statements. Thus S′ is, as it were, an ontological 'limbo' where ontological commitments are suspended for the time being, until a decision is reached. The indecision concerning ontological commitments which is thus intrinsic to S′ is a paradigm expression of ontological anxiety.

IV

THE DIFFERENTIATION THEORY OF MEANING
OF THE BUDDHIST LOGICIANS

The crucial argument for the Buddhist view that reality is not amenable to conceptualization and discourse of any kind is, it may be recalled, that the ultimate point-instants of reality defy the categories of similarity and difference which are a necessary condition for all conceptual thought. What according to the Buddhists gives rise to the similar-different polarity is ignorance of the ultimate distinctness of the point-instants. It is important here to distinguish between 'ignorance of a particular object' and 'primordial ignorance.' As ordinarily understood, 'ignorance' means ignorance of a particular object. Such ignorance necessarily presupposes some framework of knowledge in which one fails to cognize a particular object. Without such a framework it would not be possible to even talk about 'a particular object' of which one is ignorant; thus 'ignorance of a particular object' implies knowledge or the possibility of knowing. On the other hand, that which according to the Buddhists makes knowledge and all frameworks of knowledge possible is 'primordial ignorance.'[1] Thus the possibility of knowledge implies primordial ignorance, although the contrary is not necessarily true. From the viewpoint of ultimate reality, then, the similar-different polarity and all conceptual thought and knowledge based on it signalize illusion, ignorance, and negation of the true nature of reality. On the other hand, the same ignorance (i.e., 'primordial ignorance') is the foundation of conceptual knowledge and the various conceptions of reality to which conceptual knowledge gives rise.

The significance of the Buddhist view of the origin of knowledge is that the search for a cognitive link or correspondence between non-conceptual reality and conceptual thought becomes pointless, for ignorance as the origin of knowledge means that it is precisely ignorance of the true nature of reality that

1. Stcherbatsky, *Buddhist Logic*, Vol. I, p. 554.

gives rise to the belief that such a link or correspondence exists. It would also be futile and pointless to consider the object of knowledge as something independent of and separate from the act of knowing, since ignorance is a characteristic of the latter and not of reality itself or the 'objects' (i.e., point-instants) of reality. Hence the point of departure for the Buddhist theory of knowledge is 'cognition' as the fundamental act of knowing rather than the 'object' apart from cognition.

The importance of the categories of 'similarity' and 'difference' as the basis of knowledge and experience is widely recognized by both Eastern and Western philosophers. The uniqueness of the Buddhist analysis consists in that these categories are regarded as genuinely polar and thus purely conceptual in origin. In contrast, the more common view is to regard them as somehow rooted in ontology and hence as not genuinely polar but 'co-extant.' According to this view, the identity of distinct objects—however fleeting and momentary—is considered to be prior to and the basis for the subsequent conceptual elaborations. Depending on one's biases and preferences, 'similarity' or 'difference' is then given primary importance in such conceptual elaborations. Thus, for example, Karl Popper proposes that we have a "propensity to expect regularities and to search for them,"[1] and Quine explains the tendency to lump together 'similar' events in terms of a "tendency to favor most natural groupings"[2] or "to weigh qualitative differences unequally."[3] Both emphasize 'similar' over 'different,' and thus express the characteristic scientific approach to experience which, although indispensable to the success of science, is nevertheless a one-sided way of looking at the world; as Carl Jung points out: "The so-called scientific view of the world, based on this can hardly be anything more than a psychologically biased partial view which misses out all those by no means unimportant aspects that cannot be grasped statistically."[4] The psychological

1. Karl Popper, *Conjectures and Refutations*, p. 46.
2. Quine, "Identity, Ostension, and Hypostasis," *From a Logical Point of View*, p. 68.
3. Quine, *Word and Object*, p. 83.
4. C. G. Jung, "Synchronicity : An Acausal Connecting Principle," C. G. Jung and W. Pauli, *The Interpretation of Nature and the Psyche*, tr. R. F. C. Hull, Routledge & Kegan Paul, London, 1952, p. 8.

bias, however, has an ontological foundation, and it is this foundation that relieves Popper from explaining how regularities can be expected if irregularities are not observed, and Quine from accounting for the meaning of 'natural' without contrast with 'unnatural' in the so-called 'tendency to favor natural groupings.'

On the other hand, the recognition of 'similar' and different' as genuinely polar concepts means that neither is given priority over the other. Thus there can be no awareness of regularities and no grouping together of similar events if there is no perception of differences and there can be no awareness of differences if there is no perception of similarities. In view of this, the Buddhist theory of meaning is a theory of differentiation (apohavāda) which considers the similar-different polarity to be a fundamental and hence irreducible category of cognition. According to the apoha theory, "By the term 'Differentiation' what is intended is not merely a positive entity (A); nor merely the exclusion of (the other) *non-A*, but the meaning of the term is the positive thing (A) qualified by the exclusion of the other (non-A)."[1] In accordance with the irreducibility of the similar-differnt polarity, the Buddhist theory of meaning maintains the *simultaneity* of the cognition of sameness (A) and otherness (non-A), as is clear from the following illustration by Ratnakīrti : "So also from the term cow which harbours negation of non-cow, discrimination of non-cow inevitably arises simultaneously with the perception of the cow, for (the negation of non-cow) is the qualifier (of the individual)."[2] In essence, cognition of an 'object' is a cognition of the difference between sameness or similarity and otherness or difference. If this way of characterizing cognition sounds vacuous, it is not reason for embarrassment to the Buddhists. On the contrary, it gives more force and emphasis on the point which the Buddhists want to make concerning the relation between object of cognition and cognition, namely, that the object of cognition is nothing apart from the act of cognition. The vacuousness of the above statement is of the same sort as the vacuousness of the observation that "bachelors are called bachelors." The point is that

---

1. Ratnakīrti, *Apohasiddhih*, (*The Differentiation Theory of Meaning in Indian Logic*), tr. D. Sharma, Mouton, The Hague, 1969, p. 53.
    2. *Ibid.*, p. 55.

'sameness' and 'otherness' exist only because a difference is made between the two, just as there are bachelors only because some men are called so. This also shows the inappropriateness of the question: which is cognized first, A or non-A? The right question to be asked is : How does one act discriminately between A and non-A? Or how is it that one does not tie up horses when asked to tie a cow?[1] This focuses the problem upon cognition; it also suggests how the object is constituted in the discriminatory act of cognition.

The status and significance of the meaning-reference dichotomy will now be considered in the light of the Buddhist apoha theory. In the preceding chapter a distinction was made between first-order and second-order ontological statements in which the analyses of Russell and Quine terminated respectively. Both types of statements were seen to be associated with the meaning-reference dichotomy—the former by specifying that kind of entities are referents as distinct from meanings, the latter by stipulating that something whose specification depends on the particular context is a referent. These are taken as a point of departure for the Buddhist analysis. Thus the Buddhists are confronted with two questions. First, that (if anything) is the ultimate referent of a word, or, in Strawson's terminology, what in the Buddhist analysis is the 'lowest type' corresponding to Russell's 'sense-data' and Strawson's 'spatio-temporal particular'? Second, assuming that it is not possible to determine what constitutes the 'lowest type,' is it necessary to employ some (contextual) type-criterion?

The first question essentially asks whether there is a Buddhist counterpart of Russell's doctrine of the logically proper names. According to Stcherbatsky, "in the Indian view every judgment reduces to the form 'this is that,' *sa eva ayam*."[2] which is also the basic form of judgments according to Russell. Further, Stcherbatsky maintains that in the Indian, presumably including the Buddhist, view "the part 'this' refers to Reality, to the point-instant, to the 'thing in general' (Dingüberhaupt), or 'thing in itself' (svalakṣaṇa = vastu = vidhi = svarūpa).[3] This

1. Ratnakīrti, *Apohasiddhiḥ*, (*The Differentiation Theory of Meaning in Indian Logic*), tr. D. Sharma, Mouton, The Hague, 1969, p. 53.
2. Stcherbatsky, *Buddhist Logic*, Vol. II, note, p. 80.
3. *Ibid.*

suggests that the word 'this' is a logically proper name in Russell's sense, that is, it refers directly to the non-conceptual elements of reality and thus provides a link between the conceptual and the non-conceptual. Stcherbatsky himself sees a parallel between the Buddhists' point-instants and the Kantian 'a priori forms of sensibility' in that the point-instants, like the a priori forms of sensibility, determine the structure of cognition and empirical knowledge. Thus according to him, the point-instants "already contain what Kant would have called the a priori forms of our sensibility, the possibility of coordination (sārūpya), if not already some rudimentary coordination."[1] However, Stcherbatsky's interpretation seems mistaken both with respect to Kant and the Buddhists. The analogy between Kant's 'noumena' and the Buddhist 'point-instants' is plausible enough, since both represent non-conceptual and non-phenomenal ultimate reality. But in the light of the foregoing exposition and analysis of the Buddhist theory of knowledge, it is hardly conceivable how or in what sense the point-instants 'contain' the a priori forms of sensibility, especially since the latter obviously include the categories of similarity and difference. Moreover, in view of the analogy between the point-instants and noumena, Stcherbatsky is in effect saying that the noumena contain the forms of sensibility and, by implication, that there is an a priori connection not just between the forms of sensibility and experience but also between the noumena and experience; and this is certainly more than Kant himself dared to say. Kant would at most say that the relation between the noumena and experience *via* the forms of sensibility is causal. On the other hand, Russell clearly maintains that the relation between the logically proper name and sense-data is a priori, and hence Stcherbatsky's interpretation is perhaps applicable more to Russell than to Kant.

The question, however, is whether such an interpretation is also applicable to the Buddhists, as Stcherbatsky claims. The answer is not made easier by the fact that Dharmakīrti evidently uses the term 'point-instant' (svalakṣaṇa) in more than one sense, and one of the senses is *metaphorically* very concrete and particular (vyakti) object.[2] And "the term 'object' means

1. Stcherbatsky *Buddhist Logic*, Vol. II, note 6, p. 35.
2. *Ibid.*

object of cognition, i.e., an object which is cognized."[1] Also,
one finds reference in the texts the 'double character of cognition,'
such as the following :

> (Every) reality, indeed, has its real essence which is the
> particular (the unique) and a general (imagined
> aspect). That which is apprehended in direct
> perception is the unique. The object of cognition is
> really double, the *prima facie* apprehended and the
> definitely realized. (The first is) that aspect which
> appears directly (in the first moment) yadā-karam
> is an avyayībhāva = yasya ākaram anatikramya.
> (The second is the form which is constructed in a
> perceptive judgment) [yam adhyavasyati].[2]

The above passage may mislead one into thinking that there are
two temporally and logically distinct stages in cognition, namely
the 'directly perceived' and the 'distinctly cognized.' It can
then be thought of as supporting the view that the word 'this'
refers to the directly perceived unique object in the first moment
of cognition and the descriptions corresponding to the 'that'
part of the judgment refer to the constructions of the second
moment of cognition. Such a view resembles Russell's theory
of knowledge in which 'knowledge by acquaintance' consists of
immediate, non-conceptual and hence non-discriminatory,
awareness of the referent of 'this' and 'knowledge by description'
is the familiarity with the meanings of descriptive terms. If
this were also the Buddhist view, they would maintain that the
cognition of a positive entity A (the referent of 'this') comes first,
and is *subsequently* qualified by the negation of different entities
non-A, i.e., that "the perception of a cow does not involve (cognition of) others in addition to the cow itself and therefore
'Differentiation' (cow and non-cow) is a secondary judgment
based upon the force of the (primary affirmative) perception of
a cow."[3] But this view is explicitly rejected by Ratnakīrti :
"....we do not find any *successive* stages of grasping (of affirmative and negative) meaning. No one apprehends a negative
meaning, after having understood an affirmative meaning by

1. Stcherbatsky, *Buddhist Logic*, Vol. II, Dharmakīrti, *N.B.*
2. *Ibid.*, p. 34.
3. Ratnakīrti, *Apohasiddhiḥ*, p. 53.

logical implication."[1] Is there an inconsistency, then, between the 'double character' of cognition referred to in the above passage from Dharmakīrti and Ratnakīrti's insistence on the simultaneity of cognition ? In view of the apparent inconsistency, it has been suggested that the doctrine of simultaneity of cognition is a later invention in the face of criticisms against the apoha theory.[2] However, it seems more likely that an emphasis on simultaneity was required because of misunderstanding on the part of the critics, rather than because of a fault inherent in the apoha theory itself. The misunderstanding arises out of failure to distinguish between 'cognition as a process' and 'cognition as an end product of the process' or simply, 'cognition as a product.' 'Cognition' as an empirical phenomenon is a process and hence temporal like all other empirical phenomena. On the other hand, 'cognition' as an object of conceptual analysis is the product of this process. The 'object' of cognition is also such a product; for this reason the Buddhists regard 'cognition as a product' and 'object of cognition' as one and the same thing. It is with 'cognition' in the latter sense that the apoha theory is concerned. What happens temporally prior to cognition in this sense is beyond the reach of conceptual analysis and theories of meaning, for the simple reason that there is no object to talk about or analyze. However, this much can be said about cognition as a process: since cognition is a process involving temporal duration whereas ultimate reality is instantaneous, it follows that the moment of reality is always gone much before it reaches cognitive awareness. A similar situation is recognized by physicists concerning observation of astronomical phenomena. In the Buddhist view, observation of familiar earthly phenomena is in principle no different from observation of vast and distant celestial phenomena. The end result is the same : men's perceptions, whether obtained through instruments of observation such as the telescope or their own sense organs directly, are of images only, which replace the eluding moment of reality. Thus although the process of cognition begins with a direct sensation (pratyakṣa), by the time an

---

1. Ratnakīrti, *Apohasiddhiḥ* (Italics added.)
2. e.g., K. Kunjunni Raja, *Indian Theories of Meaning*, Vasanta Press, The Theosophical Society, Madras, India, 1969, p. 90.

object is distinctly cognized it is *no longer the same* : "The following is the object which is not different (it is quite similar to it). Difference here means interval in time as well as difference in quality. Thus, (every) difference (between the momentary objects) is denied."[1] The apoha theory is an analysis of the conceptual and perceptual mechanisms which produce the cognition of a distinct object.

The conceptual mechanism in question is discrimination or differentiation, which logically presupposes both 'similarity' or 'sameness' and 'difference' or 'otherness.' In cognition, therefore, the temporal simultaneity of awareness of A and non-A follows out of logical necessity from the mutual entailment of similarity and difference. One can thus say that 'A' is an object of cognition *because* it is distinguished and singled out from the rest (non-A). An 'undifferentiated, undiscriminated object' is, according to the Buddhists, a contradiction in terms, insofar as something is an object only by virtue of being distinguished and singled out from the rest. It follows that the word 'this' which has a distinct object as its referent presupposes discrimination—the awareness of 'non-this' as well as 'this.' In this respect, then, there is no difference between 'this' and other names; as Karl Potter points out, "even 'this' by itself is conceptual....in short, there are no logically proper names."[2] In fact a Buddhist might go as far as to say that the word 'this' whose sole function is to point to an object signalizes a pure act of discrimination and conceptualization.

It becomes evident now that the emphasis has been shifted from 'object of cognition' to 'cognition,' and from 'referent' to 'referend,' i.e., the instrument of reference.[3] Accordingly, the role of 'this' turns out to be that of a referend *par excellence*. But was not the issue originally in what sense, if at all, the word 'this' has a *referent* ? As pointed out above, the Buddhist analysis of 'cognition' applies equally to 'object of cognition,' the two being only different aspects of one and the same thing. Therefore the answer is ready at hand : "A word [including 'this'] denotes a mentally constructed relation of A and non-A. Thus

1. Dharmakīrti, *N.B.*, p. 26.
2. Karl Potter, *Presuppositions of India's Philosophies*, p. 189.
3. Sharma, *The Differentiation Theory of Meaning in Indian Logic*, Mouton, The Hague, 1969, Introduction, p. 26.

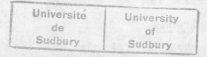

the direct import of a term is nothing other (than differentiation).[1] But it may now be objected, surely when one talks *about* something, e.g., a table, one is not talking about a relation of 'table' and 'non-table' : To get around the awkwardness of the situation, Dharmottara proposed that the referent of a word has 'quasi-externality' or 'superimposed externality.'[2] But this is hardly anything more than the trivially true observation that words or concepts purport to refer; it is certainly not to assert that words actually refer to extra-linguistic reality. But if there was any room for misunderstanding in Dharmottara's statement, it was later eliminated by Ratnakīrti who unequivocally affirms the Buddhist contention that words do not (literally) refer to external reality :

> Thus what is affirmed and denied is only the idea of an external object... (A term refers to) an external object, indeed only because of its 'feeling,' but their combination is not (externally referred to) even on the (basis of) the feeling.[3]

However, to guard against misunderstanding in the opposite direction, the Buddhists are not suggesting that when one talks *about* something, one is not really talking about anything. That names refer to objects is indeed trivially true, and the Buddhists certainly do not wish to dispute that. However, what is of interest to a theorist of cognition is how names refer or what is meant by 'reference.' It is upon such questions that the Buddhist analysis sheds new light by offering an alternative to Russell's view in which 'reference' signifies an *a priori*, hence ultimately inexplicable and mysterious, connection between a word and an external object. According to the Buddhists, there is nothing mysterious in what is man's own making, and 'reference' is man's own making insofar as it signifies an act of differentiation and a mentally constructed relation. Since 'reference' is not a connection between a word and an external object but rather a characteristic of the act of cognition, referential words (names that purport to refer) do not reveal what the object of reference ultimately is, except in the trivial sense that it is what one thinks or cognizes it to be and the 'type criterion'

1. Ratnakīrti, *Apohasiddhiḥ*, p. 99.
2. *Ibid.*, p. 93.
3. *Ibid.*, p. 91.

is therefore nothing more than an *ad hoc* device for the trivial task of determining what the object of reference is cognized to be. The type criterion is thus deprived of its ontological foundation, and this means that ontological absolutism, i.e., the commitment to first-order ontological statements, is rejected by the Buddhists.

But even if the 'lowest type' (i.e., the ultimate object of reference) and hence the meaning-reference dichotomy cannot be determined in an absolute sense, this by itself does not mean that the type criterion has no significance or that the meaning-reference dichotomy could not be maintained in the relative sense suggested by Quine. One may therefore ask whether the type criterion and the meaning-reference dichotomy are necessary even if only relative to a given context. 'Necessary' here means 'ontologically necessary' as opposed to 'logically necessary.' Something is 'logically necessary' if it follows by rules of inference from something else (which may be contingent), as for example "this book is colored" follows from "this book is red." On the other hand, what is 'ontologically necessary' need not, and usually does not, logically follow from anything else. Obviously the meaning-reference dichotomy is not thought of as the contrary, it is assumed to be basic to all statements. The 'necessity' of the meaning-reference dichotomy is thus 'ontological necessity.' For Quine, the meaning-reference dichotomy is necessary because it demarcates the boundary between what belongs to ontology (i.e., that which is capable of being a value of a bound variable, or in traditional terminology, the particular) and what does not belong to ontology (descriptions or predicates or, in traditional terminology, the universal). It moreover specifies what kind of ontology it is, namely that of particulars, even if it does not, in the case of Quine, specify what *kind* of particulars they are. Thus the universal-particular distinction parallels that of meaning-reference, and how the latter distinction is drawn depends on one's conception of the former. For example, the universalparticular distinction may be drawn between 'river' and 'the Cayster' as people are commonly inclined to do; or it may be drawn between 'the Cayster' and 'river-stage,' as Quine prefers to do.[1]

1. Quine, "Identity, Ostension, and Hypostasis," *From A Logical Point of View*, pp. 65-79.

Since the particular is nothing but the 'object' which in the analysis is inseparable from cognition, the Buddhist position concerning the distinction between the universal and the particular naturally grows out of their analysis of cognition. And in cognition, "Indeed Class and its possessor, Motion and the moving thing, Substance and Quality, or the Inherence (of the latter) in the former—are not presented to our mind as separate things." That substance and quality, universal and particular, are not cognized as separate things has been recognized by most philosophers of both East and West. Nevertheless, philosophers have insisted that they are somehow different, and as a result a hopeless epistemological dilemma has been created : On the one hand a word, e.g., 'horse' is presumed to refer to "this particular horse;" but how can the same word then be applied to the abstract idea of 'horse' which is *different* from any particular horse ? On the other hand, if the word applies to the idea because the idea is its meaning, then how can the same word apply to the particular thing horse which is certainly very different from the meaning which is the idea ? Thus the puzzled and bewildered Plato allegedly mused : "What does 'horse' mean ? A single particular horse ? No, for it may refer to *any* horse; *all* the horses, the total class ? No, for we may speak of this or that horse. But if it means neither a single horse, nor all horses, what *does* it mean ?"[2] What intrigued Plato is the problem of cognition. It therefore cannot be solved by saying that the one (the particular) exists and the other (the universal) does not. This is in effect the solution offered by the meaning-reference dichotomy. While it may help clear up ontological slums, it begs the cognitive problem.

The Buddhists, on the other hand, conclude that since no distinct stages are discernible in cognition, no ontological difference exists between the objects of cognition, the universal and the particular, but rather, "The relation of characterizing quality to a characterized Substance, this foundation of our empirical knowledge is *created by our Reason*, it is not cognized by the senses...." Therefore, "(The Buddhist view is that)

1. Vācaspatimiśra, "The Buddhist Theory of Perception," Stcherbatsky, *Buddhist Logic*, Vol. II, p. 266.
2. Friedrich Waismann, "How I See Philosophy," *Logical Positivism*, ed., A. J. Ayer, The Free Press, N.Y., 1966, p. 347.

attributes are not something apart from the substance of a thing, but *productive imagination constructs* them as something different."[1]

It was pointed out earlier that for the Buddhists, a thing is nothing over and above the qualities (dharmas) that characterize it. Now the opposite seems to hold equall : the qualities are nothing over and above the substance or thing. This shows that the Buddhists are not advocating the reduction of either things to qualities or qualities to things. They are saying that they are one and the same. In other words, the Buddhists are not concerned to assert the reality or unreality of either substance (particular) or quality (universal) but contend that the distinction between them is unreal; and to ask how the two are related—by correspondence, inherence, or causation—is just as misguided as to ask which one of them is real since the two are not separate in the first place. (An interesting consequence of this is that the Buddhist position with respect to the old dispute about universals falls, strictly speaking, outside the traditional three positions—realist, conceptualist, and nominalist. Although generally considered to be nominalists because of their doctrine of the point-instant reality, the Buddhist brand of nominalism is not what is usually understood by the term, insofar as nominalism in the usual sense asserts the reality of particulars as against universals.) But this is not to say that the Buddhists regard the universal-particular or meaning-reference distinctions themselves as false or misguided. An explanation of what the Buddhists mean by 'unreal' on the one hand and 'false' or 'misguided' on the other will make this clear. According to the Buddhists, 'real' and 'unreal' are ontological categories, and hence only the point-instants are real. Everything else is produced by 'reason' or 'imagination,' in other words, by conceptual construction, and is therefore unreal (i.e., lacks ontological basis). But what is in this sense unreal is not thereby false or misguided. False notions and misguided questions arise as a result of mistaking the unreal for the real. Thus theories of meaning and reference which assume that the distinction between universals and particulars is real (i.e., onto-

1. Vācaspatimiśra, "The Buddhist Theory of Perception," Stcherbatsky, *Buddhist Logic*, Vol. II, pp. 273, 275. (Italics added.)

logically grounded) are faulty and misguided. But it is to be noted that the falsity of the distinction between universals and particulars does not follow from the unreality of the distinction; what follows is the *contingency* of the distinction. 'Contingent' is here opposed to 'ontologically necessary,' meaning 'relative to a given viewpoint' or 'dependent on a particular conceptual framework.' Such relations as 'to the left of' and 'wiser than' are in this sense contingent. The first depends on the particular spatio-temporal viewpoint from which two objects, x and y, are viewed; the second depends on one's conception of wisdom. But there is nothing in the nature of reality, independent of such viewpoints and conceptions, which necessitates x's being to the left of y or x's being wiser than y. Nor can the possibility be ruled out of there being viewpoints or conceptual frameworks in which these relations do not obtain at all; for example, one may be watching x and y from a tree-top directly above them, or one's conception of wisdom may be such that neither x nor y is wiser than the other. The Buddhists consider the grammatical relation between 'subject' and 'predicate' which reflects the ontological distinction between particular and universal as contingent in just the same way as these relations are : it is produced by and has its foundation in nothing else than imagination and conceptual construction. Hence the Buddhists regard the subject and predicate terms as on a par with the relata in any relationships. Thus, following Quine's notation, sentences of the form 'x is y', where 'is y' is predicated of x, is rendered in the Buddhist analysis $(\exists x) (\exists y)$ Rxy, where 'R' stands for any 'relation.' This sentence has the same logical form as 'x is wiser than y,' i.e., $(\exists x) (\exists y)$ Wxy. But it now becomes obvious that the quantifier no longer serves the purpose of distinguishing subject terms from predicate terms, since the quantifier is affixed to every term. That is, 'x' can no longer be identified as the subject term by virtue of its being a bound variable any more than 'y' can, for 'y' or any other term denoting a relatum is also a bound variable. This elucidates, from the logical point of view, the Buddhist contention that the universal and the particular are in the last analysis indistinguishable. But now the quantifier becomes redundant and superfluous, since it is affixed to every term indiscriminately. The notation can therefore be simplified by replacing 'bound variables' by 'constants' which are specifiable through descriptions. Thus, to follow the previously adopted notation (according to which 'O' denotes any relation and 'f' and 'a' denote descriptions), $(\exists x)(\exists y)$ Rxy becomes O (f, a). Quine's formula $(\exists x)$ Fx can then be derived as a special case from the formula O (f, a), by substituting 'is a predicate of' for 'O'. The Buddhist formula is thus more basic than Quine's, and unlike the latter, it is capable of accommodating such languages, actual or imaginable, in which the subject-predicate structure is not assumed to reflect the basic structure of the world. Quine warns against letting a particular language dictate one's analysis of basic ontological structures and repeatedly emphasizes that logical distinctions are not to be drawn on grammatical lines.[1] However, not only how distinctions are drawn but whether they are drawn at all may be due to the influence of one's language; but this seems to have been overlooked by Quine.

The conception that has persisted in the Western tradition from Aristotle to Quine is that the primary function of statements is to predicate something of something else, and all other functions, including the expression of relations, can be expressed in terms of this primary function. Thus, in spite of criticisms (by later logicians) of Aristotle's failure to recognize relations, Aristotelian mode of thinking still persists in *meta-logic* where one talks, not about relations, but about 'dyadic predicates,' 'triadic predicates' etc. The 'something' of which something else is predicated is supposed to be an extra-linguistic, hence non-conceptual entity. Names cannot be the subjects of predicates, nor descriptions the bearers of descriptions (except in the special case where language itself is the subject of discourse); for as Quine himself has demonstrated, names as well as descriptions are construable as predicates. Thus the subject forever eludes being captured by means of names and descriptions; yet the subject is intimately and inextricably connected with the descriptions: it is neither a name nor a description but that nameless and indescribable which is named and described. Ironically enough, despite his efforts to separate logic from ontology, Quine actually ends by reaffirming the link between the two.

While the Buddhists, too, can talk about 'predicating

1. e.g., Quine, *Word and Object*, p. 16.

something of something else,' they would point out that what
underlies and makes possible such predication is not that there
is something (ontologically—this is not to say that the Buddhists
deny that there is something—but that there is cognition of
something.) Every statement of the subject-predicate form can
therefore be analyzed into descriptions of the objects of cognition and the various relations among these. For example, the
analysis of "this is a blue jar" consists of descriptions of observed
qualities, e.g., 'blue,' 'hard,' 'round,' and the relation of 'inherence,' etc.; and the word 'this' indicates that the totality of
these qualities is singled out from the rest.

It is evident by now that the problems associated with the
notions of 'meaning' and 'reference' appear in an entirely new
perspective in the light of the Buddhist analysis. Thus one cannot meaningfully say, as Quine (in the tradition of Frege and
Russell) does, that descriptions do not refer at all; for this
presupposes that something at least does refer (which is not a
description). But according to the Buddhists, descriptions are
all that one has, and therefore the question whether descriptions
refer or not cannot be even properly asked; it is analogous to
asking whether the universe as a whole is real or unreal. However, just as one may establish relative criteria within the universe
for distinguishing between 'real' and 'unreal' or even 'degrees
of reality' if one pleases, so also one can establish relative criteria
for distinguishing between words that refer and those that do
not. And Quine would have no quarrel with this. Wherein,
then, lies the difference between Quine and the Buddhist
logicians ? The difference lies in their respective analyses
underlying the common conclusion concerning the relativity
of the meaning-reference dichotomy. Quine's acceptance of the
second-order ontological statement grows out of a fundamentally
dualistic framework of words and things, language and experience, and finally meaning and reference. On the other hand,
his rejection, or rather suspension, of commitment to a first-
order ontological statement is a result of his recognition that
the choice of ontological assumptions can only be justified relative
to a particular set of pragmatic goals and aims. Quine's position then is to use the previous analogy, that of firmly maintaining
that the universe is divided into the real and the unreal while
at the same time admitting that it is not in anybody's power to

know exactly how and where the dividing line is drawn. Quine's thesis of ontological relativism rests on empirical evidence—the fact that the aims and goals which in the last analysis justify ontological commitments vary from person to person, from community to community. The question whether it is *logically* impossible to obtain anything but relative justification for ontological assumptions, stumbles on the dualism and sharp dichotomy of meaning and reference, and remains forever unanswered. One may be eager to place one's hands on the bare referent, but unfortunately one can never know for certain whether one really succeeds in doing so. Preoccupation with the successes and failures of such endeavors, however, is regarded by most tough-minded logicians as a sign of morbidity which should be allowed no place in the sober pursuits of logical analysis. But it seldom occurs to the logicians that the root cause of the morbidity may lie in the so-called sober analysis itself.

The Buddhist logicians' differentiation theory of meaning shows not only that justification of ontological assumptions is relative but that it is necessarily so. Their analysis of language and experience, words and things, and meaning and reference shows that behind the apparent dichotomy there is an interpenetration and inseparateness of the two aspects in cognition. Thus the dualistic paradigm gives way to a non-dualistic one in which the act of cognition is the fundamental unit. The apparent dichotomy of concepts and things, meanings and referents, dissolves into a dialectical unity, in which "words are derived from concepts and vice versa, concepts are derived from words,"[1] and "Subject-predicate relation is but dialectical."[2] Differentiation encompasses both the act of referring and identification of meaning in cognition.

---

1. Skr. vikalpa-yonayaḥ śabdāḥ vikalpāḥ śabdayonayaḥ, (Dignāga) Ratnakīrti, *Apohasiddhiḥ*, p. 15.
2. Skr. saṁvṛttisad eva dharmi-dharmalakṣaṇam, *Ibid*.

V

QUINE ON THE ANALYTIC AND THE SYNTHETIC

The belief that every statement falls into one or the other of the two mutually exclusive and jointly exhaustive classes, the analytic and the synthetic, has been one of the cornerstones of the Western philosophical tradition. As is often the case with fundamental beliefs, the analytic-synthetic distinction was hardly noticed, much less questioned, until it was finally subjected to scrutiny and criticism. It is only then that it suddenly became a topic of heated controversy. By contrast, the analytic-synthetic distinction as an issue of serious importance or controversy has been conspicuously absent in the history of Indian philosophy, both the Brahmanical and Buddhist traditions.[1] A Western observer, speculating on the reasons for what may appear to him a serious negligence or perhaps even insensitivity on the part of the Indian philosophers toward fundamental philosophical problems, is naturally tempted either to conclude that the Indian philosophers simply failed to recognize the analytic-synthetic distinction; or, if he is sympathetically inclined, to try to show that the Indians did, after all, draw the analytic-synthetic distinction although they did not give as much emphasis to it as the Westerners did. Both interpretations reflect a Western bias, namely, the assumption that there is a distinction between the analytic and the synthetic, whether or not one recognizes it. This assumption, however, is in general not shared by the Indian philosophers, and hence the first interpretation is wrong in attributing to the Indians a failure to recognize a problem where, from their point of view, there is no problem to be recognized; and the second is also likely to be wrong in being too eager to look for parallels and similarities between the Western and Indian positions where none may exist.

The Buddhist logicians' position concerning the analytic-synthetic distinction grows out of their general analysis of con-

---

1. Potter, *Presuppositions of India's Philosophies*, p. 66.

ceptual-empirical knowledge and reality. As shown previously, this involves a rejection of the meaning-reference dichotomy as a fundamental feature of knowledge and reality. The analytic-synthetic distinction, on the other hand, is rooted in the meaning-reference dichotomy, and whereas both are central tenets of the Western philosophical tradition, neither is given such a position in the Buddhist philosophical analysis. It would therefore be misleading to say that the Buddhists fail to recognize the analytic-synthetic distinction insofar as this implies that they have missed something which in their scheme of things does not even exist.   On the other hand, it would be equally misleading to say that the Buddhists recognize the analytic-synthetic distinction, for the problem of analyticity as it is known in the West simply does not arise in the Buddhist framework.

     If it is indeed true that the analytic-synthetic distinction is not recognized by the Buddhists, one wonders as to what it means to compare the Buddhist and Western philosophies on this issue.   There are two levels at which any thesis or problem, including the analytic-synthetic distinction, can be appraised. First, one may examine the various formulations of the problem and the solutions proposed to it.   Second, one may examine the nature of the problem itself, that is, whether or not it is a genuine problem. In the Western tradition, Quine has pioneered the attacks which have threatened, and, according to many philosophers, succeeded in demolishing the analytic-synthetic distinction.   But while Quine offers a thorough analysis of the problem of analyticity at the first level, he does not carry the analysis far and deep enough to examine the problem at the second level.   In other words, although Quine shows that all attempts to provide adequate criteria for analyticity fail, he neither shows nor asks *why* they fail.   It will be maintained here that the analytic-synthetic distinction is generated out of a dualism which, whether it is called dualism of 'meaning and reference', 'language and fact', or 'conceptual and non-conceptual', is regarded as ultimate and in this sense 'ontological'.   Such a dualism is not only a necessary condition for the analytic-synthetic distinction but also a sufficient condition for the possibility of establishing criteria for analyticity. That is, while ontological dualism does not guarantee that a criterion will actually be found, it ensures the possibility of finding one; in short, it guarantees that the problem of analyticity is a genuine problem. Conversely, were dualism to break down at a fundamental level, the analytic-synthetic distinction would thereby also collapse, and the problem of finding criteria for analyticity not only remains unsolved but actually becomes insoluble; it becomes, in other words, a pseudo-problem. Naturally, the problem of analyticity does not and cannot arise in the first place in a non-dualistic framework, such as that of the Buddhist logicians. It will be shown that Quine's analysis is not carried far enough because of the ambivalence of his position concerning dualism. Thus, despite his criticisms of the various species of dualism, including the analytic-synthetic distinction, Quine seems to adhere to a dualism at a basic level (generic duailsm). For this reason it is not clear which of the two positions Quine finally adopts: whether he considers the problem of analyticity a pseudo-problem, or whether he sides with dualism. But one thing is clear: Quine must choose one and reject the other; he cannot at the same time accept dualism and regard the problem of analyticity as a pseudo-problem. For, as will be shown in the sequel, there is a logical connection between dualism and the problem of analyticity such that one cannot at the same time reject dualism and consider the problem of analyticity to be genuine or conversely, accept dualism and consider the problem of analyticity to be a pseudo-problem. Showing the logical connection between the problem of analyticity and dualism requires a non-dualistic viewpoint, and such is provided by the Buddhist logicians. It will also become clear that an answer to the question, why does the problem of analyticity not arise in a non-dualistic framework, is also the answer to the question, why it arises in a dualistic framework.

In the present chapter, the traditional conception of the analytic-synthetic distinction as it arises from the meaning-reference dichotomy will be briefly outlined, followed by a detailed examination of Quine's formulation and criticism of the problem of analyticity. The latter consists of a presentation of Quine's analysis and an examination of his conclusions concerning the analytic-synthetic distinction as a species of dualism as well as a dualism at the fundamental or generic level. A formal analysis will then be undertaken to show, first, that the quest of a criterion of analyticity is generically a quest for a criterion of identity (i.e., irrespective of the entities whose identity is in concern), and secondly, that a quest for a criterion of identity presupposes generic dualism (i.e., irrespective of a system's ultimate categories.) In the last chapter, the problem of analyticity will be explored from the non-dualistic viewpoint of the Buddhist logicians, in which the Buddhist analysis of the problem of analyticity as a pseudo-problem will be seen to emerge as a radical alternative to Quine's more moderate proposal to merely deny all solutions to the problem.

The meaning-reference dichotomy postulates two fundamental categories of entities, the conceptual or linguistic (meaning) and the non-conceptual or factual (reference) which serve as the bases of conceptual-empirical knowledge. Broadly speaking, conceptual-empirical knowledge is the result of a synthesis of the conceptual and non-conceptual elements, as is manifest in the formula $(\exists x)\ Fx$. One can thus imagine two extreme situations where one or the other element is missing and where consequently there is not synthesis. For instance, if the conceptual element is missing, one may behold 'pure fact' but one has no means of conveying information about it; on the other hand, if the non-conceptual element is absent, one has the means, but nothing about which to convey information. In either case, conceptual-empirical knowledge would be impossible. One may further observe that there are no statements corresponding to the former situation because the materials and tools for constructing statements are totally lacking. On the other hand, there are statements corresponding to the latter situation, but they are not about the world. If they can be said to be about anything at all, they are about the words that occur in them. Thus their truth is determined solely on the basis of the conceptual elements constituting them, as opposed to genuinely synthetic statements whose truth at least in part depends on the facts they are about. The former statements are called 'analytic' as opposed to 'synthetic.' These differences between analytic and synthetic statements are commonly expressed by saying that analytic statements are true by virtue of the meanings of their terms,[1] whereas synthetic statements are true or false by virtue

---

1. White, *Toward Reunion in Philosophy*, p. 104.

of their referents. This suggests a parallel between the meaning-reference dichotomy and the analytic-synthetic distinction:
The central problem of the former is to explicate and find criteria
for 'referent' independently of considerations of meaning, while
the problem of the latter is to find criteria for analyticity without
recourse to 'referents.' However, pursuing the parallel a little
further seems to result in a dilemma: If the criterion of analyticity depends on the criterion of meaning, the question naturally
arises: what sort of entities are meanings, just as it was previously
asked, what sort of entities are referents? Such a question
implies that 'meanings' have ontological status of their own,
just as 'referents' have. But the very purpose of the meaning-
reference dichotomy was to enable one to draw the boundaries
of ontology so as to exclude meanings from ontology. It now
seems, however, that the meaning-reference dichotomy merely
divides the domain of ontology into two parts which accommo-
dates both meanings and referents, thereby flatly defeating the
original purpose of the meaning-reference dichotomy.

Quine does not believe that the above dilemma is a genuine
one, but believes that it can be avoided by reformulating the
problem of analyticity in accordance with the precept of the
meaning-reference dichotomy. Thus the question, what sort
of entities are meanings? is misguided and, according to Quine,
a hang-over from the earlier irresponsible claims of realism. "A
felt need for meant entities may derive from an earlier failure to
appreciate that meaning and reference are distinct."[1] Similarly,
the view that the notion of 'analyticity' depends on that of 'meaning', and hence, that the clarification of analyticity presupposes
the clarification of meaning, needs to be radically revised. According to Quine, it is not that 'analyticity depends on 'meaning'
but rather, a criterion of meaning emerges from, and is clarified
in terms of 'analyticity'. In this way, Quine hopes, the linger-
ing conception of meanings as entities in their own right will
at last vanish:

> Once the theory of meaning is sharply separated from the
> theory of reference, it is a short step to recognize as the
> primary business of the theory of meaning simply the

    1. Quine, "Two Dogmas of Empiricism," *From a Logical Point of View,*
p. 22.

synonymy of linguistic forms and the analyticity of statements; meanings themselves as obscure intermediary
entities, may well be abandoned.[1]

In view of the meaning-reference dichotomy, then the problem
of analyticity acquires a new formulation in which it no longer
presupposes the notion of 'meaning' but rather the latter can be
explicated in terms of 'analyticity'. The traditional Kantian
conception of analyticity rested on the idea that concepts or
meanings somehow exist ready-made, and all one had to do
was to find those meanings that are identical or contained in one
another. But now the assumption of ready-made meanings is
seen to be both unwarranted and unnecessary. In Quine's
formulation, 'analyticity' is to be explained solely in terms of
'synonymy of linguistic forms', without appeal to mysterious,
unobservable 'meanings', and 'sameness of meaning' can be
explicated in terms of such synonymy.

But if the traditional approach to the problem of analyticity with its unwarranted assumptions was less than satisfactory,
the new, rigorous approach meets with total failure—as shown
by none other than Quine himself. What Quine does not show,
however, is *why* the attempts to find a criterion of analyticity
fail—whether the attempts have so far been simply inadequate
or whether the task itself is impossible; in short, whether or not
the problem of analyticity is a pseudo-problem. But before
considering this question, Quine's formulation of the problem of
analyticity and his criticism of it will be examined in some detail.

Following Quine's suggestion, 'analyticity' is, broadly
speaking, a function of a certain relationship between 'linguistic
forms'. By 'linguistic forms' one may simply understand either
a visual or auditory sign, i.e., a written or spoken word or behavioral responses equivalent to such a sign. Thus both relata
are observable entities or events, and the problem of analyticity consists in establishing an explicit criterion whereby the
relationship on which analyticity depends can be said to hold
among the relata. By contrast, in the traditional formulation
the relata are unobservable, obscure entities and hence a criterion
of the relationship could be no less unobservable and obscure.

1. Quine, "Two Dogmas of Empiricism", *From a Logical Point of
View*, P. 22

The important question, then, is what is the relationship between two linguistic forms that lies at the basis of analyticity ? The answer is found by considering the standard form of an analytic statement: 'A is A.' The relationship between the linguistic forms which constitute the subject and predicate terms is clearly one of identity. Thus a statement whose subject and object terms are identical is an analytic statement. For example, "a bachelor is a bachelor" is an analytic statement. However, not all analytic statements have the form 'A is A'; for instance, "a bachelor is an unmarried man" has the form 'A is B' although it is regarded as analytic. The problem of analyticity, therefore, consists in finding a criterion whereby implicitly analytic statements of the form 'A is B' can be reduced to explicitly analytic statements of the form 'A is A'. Such a criterion would then justify the reduction of certain apparently non-identical linguistic forms (A and B) to identical linguistic forms (A and A) by allowing a substitution of A for B. Words which can be substituted for one another are said to be synonymous, and thus the problem of analyticity becomes a problem of clarifying and finding criteria of 'synonymy'.

The problem of analyticity as outlined here avoids ontological issues, such as whether or not meanings exist over and above linguistic forms or words. It is to be noted, however, that finding a criterion for analyticity is not simply a logical problem; for the reason there is a problem of analyticity at all is precisely that there exists a class of analytic statements which cannot be derived from or reduced to explicitly analytic statements by means of rules of logic alone. One needs besides the strictly formal criteria provided by rules of logic non-formal, i.e. cognitive criteria. In view of these considerations an exposition and examination of Quine's criticism of the attempts to solve the problem of analyticity is in order.

Quine considers three approaches to the problem of analyticity, which correspond to the following definitions of 'analyticity' :

(1) A statement s is analytic if and only if 'p' is *defined* as 'q' (where 'p' and 'q' are the subject and predicate terms of s).

(2) A statement s is analytic if and only if 'p' is interchangeable *salva veritate* with 'q'.

(3)   A statement s is analytic if and only if it is true by a semantical rule.

The first definition proposes that synonymy is a matter of definition. Thus 'bachelor' and 'unmarried man' are synonymous because 'bachelor' is defined as 'unmarried man'. However, this merely illuminates the formal or logical character of the relation between two words which are said to be synonymous whereas the real question is, how does one know that 'bachelor' and 'unmarried man' are in fact defined in terms of each other, or what amounts to the same question, according to what criterion is 'bachelor' defined as 'unmarried man' rather than as something else?

Two approaches to answering this question have been proposed. First, one may simply consult a dictionary in order to verify that 'bachelor' is indeed defined as 'unmarried man'. But then one is appealing to empirical facts—in this case the speech habits of a given linguistic community (which, incidentally, is the sole source of information of the lexicographer and hence no additional help can be gotten from him). If definitions are indeed based on common usages of words and nothing else, finding criteria of synonymy becomes a matter of empirical investigation, in which case whatever criterion one may come by, it will not help to clarify the distinction between the analytic and the synthetic; if anything, it may obliterate and eliminate the distinction altogether.

But it may now be insisted that although the dictionary definitions are discovered and collected by empirical means, the definitions themselves rest on pre-existing synonymies. However, even though the distinction between the analytic and the synthetic may thus be saved, one has not made one inch of progress toward explaining, let alone providing cognitive criterion for synonymy and analyticity.

The other approach is to say that definitions and hence synonymies are simply created. Thus, for example, one may explicitly introduce a new notation for purposes of abbreviation. There is then no need to consult either dictionaries or lexicographers; and moreover, one can be sure that the definition does not rest on pre-existing synonymies. However, although some cases of synonymy are known to be created by definition, there are a vast number of others which are *not* known to be so created.

(This observation concerns the limitations and uncertainty of the state of knowledge at any given time and is not to be mistaken as implying that synonyms are *known* not to have been created by definition. The latter claim is obviously not true, but the former is and is sufficient to show just how much expressly created definitions help to explain and provide criterion for cognitive synonymy in general.) Even if one wants to dogmatically adhere to the absurd thesis that all definitions were created by someone or other at some time or other, such a thesis is no more and no less helpful in providing criteria for cognitive synonymy than the view that definitions rest on pre-existing synonymies. In either case Quine's observation holds, namely that "definitions rest on synonymy rather than explaining it."[1]

According to the second definition of 'analytic statement' a statement is analytic if and only if the subject and predicate terms are interchangeable without affecting the truth value of the statement. Now it is obvious that the definiens and the definiendum are always in this sense interchangeable, for this is precisely what a definition stipulates. In view of the foregoing difficulties, it would therefore be pointless to offer interchangeability as a criterion of synonymy unless it can be shown to be independent of 'definition'. The interchangeability criterion is therefore strengthened by the *salva veritate* clause which requires that interchangeability obtain in all possible worlds, regardless of how words happen to be defined in the actual world. But this is nothing but the Leibnizian notion of 'necessity' which thus finds its way back to the notion of 'analyticity'. That 'bachelor' and 'unmarried man' are interchangeable *salva veritate* is then conveyed by saying that the statement "all and only bachelors are unmarried men" is not just true but necessarily true. However, the shortcomings of this proposal are evident as soon as it is asked, how is one to know whether a given statement is necessarily true or just true? It is not at all obvious why the statement "all and only bachelors are unmarried men" should be considered necessarily true and the statement "all and only living beings are mortal" true only with a high degree of probability, rather than the other way round. The mystery of analyticity now rests sealed in the notion of 'necessity' and

1. Quine, "Two Dogmas of Empiricism", *From a Logical Point of View*, p. 26.

it is therefore of no avail to say that the predicate 'necessarily' applies only to analytic statements.

The notion of interchangeability, however, suggests another direction in which criteria for analyticity may be sought without appeal to either 'definition' or 'necessity'. One can imagine a language in which the predicate terms have no other function than to group objects into classes. The sole criterion of 'meaning' in such a language consists of the extensions of words, i.e., the class of objects denoted by the word. Any two words which have identical extensions are then interchangeable *salva veritate*,[1] and synonymy and hence analyticity are determined simply by checking whether the extensions of the subject and predicate terms are identical. Unfortunately, however, there is only one method for checking the identity of extensions, namely that of the lexicographer, and Quine points out once again that such a method cannot guarantee

> that the extensional agreement of 'bachelor' and 'unmarried man' rests on meaning rather than merely on accidental matters of fact, as does the extensional agreement of 'creature with a heart' and 'creature with kidneys'.[2]

Hence Quine concludes that "the fact remains that extensional agreement falls short of cognitive synonymy of the type required for explaining analyticity...."[3]

The third and last proposal attempts to explain analyticity in terms of the notion of 'semantical rule'. This proposal differs from the previous two in that it tries to clarify and establish criteria for analyticity within the context of a particular language rather than independently of such a context as the other proposals did. Accordingly, analyticity is construed as a relation between a language L and a statement S rather than as a property of S. The problem, then, is to make sense of this relation generally for the variables 'L' and 'S'.[4] Instead of appealing to such dubious, unexplained notions as 'definition' or 'necessity', the criterion may now be sought in the explicit characteristics of L, namely the semantical rules of L. Thus a semantical rule of L_0

1. Quine, "Two Dogmas of Empiricism," *From a Logical Point of View*, p. 30.
2. *Ibid.*, p. 31.
3. *Ibid.*
4. *Ibid.*, p. 33.

which states that and "such and such statements and only
those are analytic in L_o." enables one to pick out the analytic
statements of L_o. However, such a rule can hardly be said to explain 'analyticity' as it simply appeals to the unexplained word
'analytic'. This is, however, not a serious difficulty, for the rule
can be reformulated as follows: "such and such statements are in-
cluded among the true statements of L_o." it being understood that
there may be other true statements in L_o which are not specified
by the semantical rule. Here the word 'analytic' does not appear
in the statement of the rule. The difference between analytic
statements and other kinds of statements is then that analytic
statements are true according to a semantical rule, whereas other
statements are simply true.[1]

But what is one to understand by the notion of 'semantical
rule' ? It seems to be as much in need of clarification as the
notion of 'analyticity' which it is supposed to explain. It may
be maintained, however, that the unexplained term 'semantical
rule' can be excused because, unlike the words 'synonymy',
'necessity', etc., the word 'semantical rule' has clear and un-
ambiguous extensional meaning in the context of a particular
language, namely, the list of semantical rules of the language.
But this proposal is not spared from Quine's criticism either.
Thus Quine once again draws attention to the difficulties inherent in extensional meaning. What is listed under the head-
ing 'Semantical Rules of L_o' applies only to Lo and no other
language, and hence the analyticity conferred by means of the
rules also applies only to L_o. Therefore, if one wishes to find
out which statements are analytic in L_1 or L_2 the list of semantical rules of L_0 is of no avail; one must consult the lists under
'Semantical Rules of L_1, 'Semantical Rules of L_2', etc. By such a
procedure one could at best establish criteria of 'analytic-for-L ',
'analytic-for-L_2', etc., but not generally for the relation 'analytic
for'. For, as Quine points out, the relative term 'semantical
rule of' is yet to be clarified. Quine does not point out, although
it is obvious, that unless the word 'semantical rule' has inten-
sional meaning as well as extentional, one may continue col-
lecting lists of semantical rules indefinitely without ever arriving
at general criteria of 'semantical rule'. There is yet another

---

1. Quine, "Two Dogmas of Empiricism," *From a Logical Point of
View.* p. 34.

and more devastating criticism which Quine does not make but which highlights the utter unsuitability of extensional meaning as a candidate for criterion of analyticity. This is simply the point that consulting a list of semantical rules is in principle no different from consulting a dictionary or a lexicographer; in other words, being a semantical rule is just as much dependent on accidental matters of fact—on being listed under 'Semantical Rules of— '—as extensional agreement of words or the lexicographer's definitions are.

It may be objected, however, that there is a difference between taking about 'analytic-for-L_0' and talking about 'analyticity' for L_0, and that the latter is not dependent on empirical facts because the designing and discovery of semantical rules of L_0 falls outside the scope of L_0 itself. But if this is so, then the explanation of these rules as well as of 'analyticity' also fall outside of L_0; and one is back where one started: searching for explanation and criterion of analyticity.

As a last desperate effort to save what little there is to be saved of the prospects to find criterion of analyticity, it may be conceded that 'semantical rule' and 'analyticity' cannot be explicated in the case of natural languages since their semantical rules may not be readily identifiable and distinguishable from other kinds of statements, but that in the case of artificial languages which contain sets of explicit semantical rules the problem of understanding the notion of 'semantical rule' may be solved as follows. One may construct what may be called a 'meta-semantical rule' to govern all artificial languages, which states that any L as a whole constitutes an ordered pair and by 'semantical rule of L' is "meant" the second component of the pair L. Such a meta-semantical rule provides a general criterion of 'semantical rule' which applies to any L. This solution, however, is not without resemblance to one which was considered earlier, according to which the problem of finding criterion of analyticity was simply made to disappear by creating synonymies by definition. In the present case the problem could be actually made to disappear even faster by construing L outright as an ordered pair whose second component is the class of its analytic statements. At this point, however, it might be wiser to follow

Quine's recommendation and "just stop tugging at our boot-straps altogether."[1]

This concludes Quine's critique of the problem of analyti-city. According to him, "for all its a priori reasonableness, a boundary between analytic and synthetic statements simply has not been drawn. That there is such a distinction to be drawn at all is an unempirical dogma of the empiricists, a metaphysical article of faith."[2]

Quine's analysis has shown the indefensibility of the analytic-synthetic dualism. This dualism, however, is rooted in a more fundamental dualism, and there is no reason why the analysis should stop short of reaching the roots. It is therefore strange that Quine who has rejected dualism as concerns in-dividual statements should reaffirm dualism at another level where statements are considered collectively. Thus while he concludes "that it is nonsense, and the root of much nonsense, to speak of a linguistic and factual component in the truth of any individual statement," he goes on to add: "Taken col-lectively, science has its double dependence upon language and experience; but this duality is not significantly traceable into the statements of science taken one by one."[3] However, Quine's conclusion is but a reiteration of his position concern-ing the meaning-reference dichotomy. It will be recalled that while Quine denied that language and conceptual means can ever reach the purely extra-linguistic and non-conceptual 'referent', he nevertheless continued to adhere to the meaning-reference dichotomy which posits a distinction between the con-ceptual and the non-conceptual. But the meaning-reference dichotomy is nothing but the language-experience dualism which Quine is here affirming. Quine is himself aware of the two dualisms being actually two sides of one and the same coin. Thus he observes that the analytic-synthetic distinction is really a twofold dogma: if there is no sharp division between the analytic and the synthetic, then not only are there no analytic statements whose truth depends on their linguistic components alone, but also there are no synthetic statements whose truth depends solely on their factual content. Thus the verifiability theory of mean-

1. Quine, "Two Dogmas of Empiricism," *From a Logical Point of View.* p. 36.
2. *Ibid.*, p. 41.
3. *Ibid.*, p. 42.

ing falls with the analytic-synthetic distinction, for "the two dogmas are indeed at root identical."[1] The verifiability theory of meaning is based on the assumption that names have solely extra-linguistic referents, which Quine has shown to be unfounded for exactly the same reason as the analytic-synthetic distinction. Thus the theory of extra-linguistic referents, the verifiability theory of meaning, and the analytic-synthetic distinction all stand or fall with the same assumption, namely that two components, factual and linguistic, are distinguishable in statements which constitute conceptual-empirical knowledge. Nevertheless, Quine wants to preserve the fact-language dichotomy at the basis of knowledge. For while denying the existence of a criterion for drawing a boundary between the factual and linguistic components with respect to individual statements, he seems to affirm the dichotomy with respect to the collection of statements called 'scientific knowledge'.[2] One wonders, however, whether the fact-language dualism is any more discernible in collections of statements than in individual statements. If anything, the chances of discerning it in a collection of statements seem far slimmer than discerning it in individual statements, simply because the former are much less determinate entities than the latter. Therefore, dualism with respect to collections of statements is a much more sweeping metaphysical dogma than that with respect to individual statements.

It may appear at first glance self-contradictory on the one hand to deny, as Quine seems to do, that there is a distinction to be drawn between the factual and the linguistic, and on the other hand to affirm that knowledge ultimately consists of these two components. There is, however, no contradiction here, if the two statements are considered as belonging to different ontological orders. Two statements belong to different ontological orders if and only if one entails the other but not vice versa. Thus the first statement which Quine denies asserts that "there is a distinction to be drawn between the factual and the linguistic according to such-and-such criterion," and the second statement which Quine affirms asserts that "there is a distinction between the factual and the linguistic, whether or not a criterion for

1. Quine, "Two Dogmas of Empiricism," *From a Logical point of View*. p. 41.

2. Similarly, it may be recalled that despite his denial that a criterion of 'referent' exists, Quine affirmed the meaning-reference dichotomy at the basis of knowledge.

drawing the distinction can be found." It is obvious that the first statement entails the second but not vice versa. There is therefore no contradiction in affirming the latter while denying the former. According to the distinction between first-order ontological statements (S) and second-order ontological statements (S') (pp. 41-43), the statement "there is a distinction to be drawn between the factual and the linguistic according to such-and-such criterion" is a first-order ontological statement, or simply S, and the statement "there is a distinction between the factual and the linguistic, whether or not a criterion for drawing the distinction can be found" is a second-order ontological statement, or S'. Quine's criticism of the analytic-synthetic distinction amounts to a rejection of S on grounds that no criterion of analyticity, which is required for drawing the fact-language dichotomy, has been established. But Quine is not thereby compelled to reject S' which asserts that conceptual-empirical knowledge ultimately consists of the factual and linguistic components, for S' is compatible with both S and its denial. Moreover, S' is compatible with the view that there are several different ways of drawing the fact-language dichotomy, depending on the needs and purposes at hand. Thus Quine can resolve the problem of analyticity by adopting the standpoint of relativism and pragmatism.

However, the problem of analyticity (as formulated by Quine) can be dissolved by showing it to be a pseudo-problem. For the roots of the analytic-synthetic distinction lie not in S as Quine assumes but far deeper in S'. In other words, the possibility of *finding* a criterion for analyticity (S) depends on there actually *being* a distinction between the factual and the linguistic components of knowledge (S'). Thus S' *asserts* ontological dualism while S only entails it, and it is easy to see therefore that the rejection of S does not logically compel the rejection of S'. However, the rejection of S' does entail the impossibility of S. In other words, given a non-dualistic ontology, the epistemological claim that dualism is discernible (S) is necessarily false; all attempts to establish S are futile and, by the same token, all attempts to refute it are spurious. In short, S and therewith the problem of analyticity are pseudo-problems. It will be shown that Quine's formulation and criticism of the problem of analyticity presuppose a non-dualistic framework and therefore Quine has (unwittingly) shown the problem of analyticity to be a pseudo-problem. But to acknowledge that the problem of analyticity is a pseudo-problem is to reject ontological dualism (S'), and conversely, to regard the problem of analyticity as a genuine problem is to commit oneself to ontological dualism. Therefore, Quine should either reformulate the problem of analyticity within a dualistic framework or reject not only the analytic-synthetic distinction but also ontological dualism.

The necessary connection between the search for a criterion of analyticity and the presupposition of dualism can be shown by examining the internal logic of 'identity'. For, as will be shown, the notion of analyticity ultimately rests on 'identity', regardless of what other assumptions may be adopted or rejected in formulating the problem of analyticity. Such formulations differ from the traditional conception of analyticity in terms of 'sameness of meaning' only because they may deny certain assumptions concerning the notion of 'meaning' but not because they give up the idea that 'analyticity' has to do with 'sameness'.

The difficulties associated with the notion of 'sameness' or 'identity' are familiar in the history of philosophy. Thus the paradoxical nature of questions concerning identity is implicit in Leibniz's principle of the identity of indiscernibles, which states that "if two things are identical, they are indiscernible from one another and hence not two distinct things; on the other hand, if they are discernible as two distinct things, they are not identical." Leibniz's principle in effect says that one cannot significantly ask whether two things are identical. For this reason, Wittgenstein declared in the *Tractatus*: " . . . to say of *two* things that they are identical is nonsense, and to say of *one* thing that it is identical with itself is to say nothing at all."[1]

It may appear surprising, then, that the problem of identity under various guises has continued to preoccupy philosophers although one cannot even *significantly* ask questions concerning the identity of two entities. The reason is that the analyses of Leibniz and Wittgenstein have shown problems of identity to be paradoxical and nonsensical within non-dualistic frameworks, whereas the problem of identity has persisted because dualistic modes of thinking have persisted. Thus it appears that the

1. Wittgenstein, *Tractatus Logico-Philosophicus*, p. 105.

question of identity can be significantly raised within a dualistic
framework.   The connection between questions involving identity on the one hand and dualism or non-dualism on the other
therefore needs to be examined in some detail.   But first what
is meant by 'ontological dualism', 'dualistic framework', or
simply 'dualism', and 'ontological non-dualism', 'non-dualistic
framework', or 'non-dualism' will be clarified.

Dualism assumes at least two ontologically distinct categories of entities.   Two entities belong to distinct ontological
categories if the criterion which an entity must satisfy in order
that it may be said to exist is different in each case; and conversely, two entities belong to the same ontological category if they
satisfy the same criterion of 'existence'. Assuming, for instance,
that public verifiability is the criterion of existence, then while
'physical events' exist according to this criterion, 'mental events'
do not.   'Physical events' and 'mental events' belong to different
ontological categories, and if both kinds of events are to exist,
some other criterion of existence is required besides public verifiability.   According to the criterion of verifiability, 'meanings'
and 'linguistic forms' (as defined on p. 70) belong to distinct
ontological categories, whereas 'physical events' and 'linguistic
forms' belong to the same ontological category. Thus a world-
view, framework, or ontology which considers both 'physical
events' and 'mental events' or both 'linguistic forms' and 'physical
events' as legitimate, irreducible entities is dualistic, whereas a
world-view which admits both 'physical events' and 'linguistic
forms' is not on that account dualistic.

What happens to the notion of 'identity' in a non-dualistic
framework on the one hand and a dualistic framework on the
other will be illustrated by means of the example of two persons
who are thinking about the same thing.   This example is parti-
cularly instructive because it is the very same example which
puzzled Frege and led him to posit a dualism which subsequently
came to be known as the meaning-reference dichotomy.   Frege
held that the only way one could successfully explain the phrase
"two persons are thinking about the same thing" was to consider
the object of thought as belonging to a category different from
both 'mental events' and 'physical events', so that the objects of
thought (which Frege calls 'concepts') are "neither things of the
outer world nor ideas."   The following considerations will

show, however, that a dualism, whether of objects of thought versus physical events or objects of thought versus mental events, is *implicit* in the phrase "two persons are thinking about the same thing" and hence the determination to 'successfully' explain the phrase betrays a prior commitment to dualism. On the other hand, if dualism is not assumed, the phrase "two persons are thinking about the same thing" cannot escape Leibniz's paradox.

Thus consider, first, an analysis of the statement "Two persons, A and B, are thinking about the same thing, p" in a non-dualistic framework. Assuming that the only ontological category is that of 'mental events', then both 'objects of thought' and 'persons having thoughts' are ultimately reducible to 'mental events'. In other words, 'objects' are nothing over and above the mental events in which they occur, and similarly 'persons' are nothing over and above the mental states which occur in them. This is not to say that persons and objects disappear or are transformed into something ethereal. What is meant by 'physical events', such as persons and objects, being reducible to 'mental events' is simply that there is nothing in the descriptions of persons or objects which compels one to assign them to the ontological category 'physical event' rather than the ontological category 'mental event'. Thus, let 'Ap' denote the event 'A is thinking of p' and '=' denote identity. Since the ultimate ontological category is that of 'mental events', Ap is a mental event. Objects and persons are then reduced to mental events as follows: A=Ap and p=Ap, and therefore A=p. Similarly, let the event 'B is thinking of p' be denoted by 'Bp', it can then be analyzed into B=Bp and p=Bp, and therefore B=p. But if A=p and B=p, then obviously A=B. And it is clear now that one cannot ask without paradox whether two distinct persons are thinking about the same thing, since there are here no two distinct persons in the first place. (There is only a series of descriptions, but nothing to indicate which segment or portion of the series belongs to A and which belongs to B.) Furthermore, not only A is indistinguishable from B but also p is indistinguishable from A and B, and hence the question whether two persons are thinking about the same thing reduces to the tautologous question whether a mental state is identical with itself.

The analysis is essentially the same if one chooses "physical event' as the single ontological category. One and the same criterion (e.g. public verifiability) will then be applied uniformly to 'persons having thoughts' as well as 'objects of thought'. One and the same set of descriptions of the visible and audible signs (which constitute the stimuli and verbal responses of A) therefore exhausts the descriptions of A, p, and Ap. Similarly, one and the same set of descriptions exhausts B, p, and Bp. The paradox arises when one asks whether the two sets of descriptions are identical. If they are identical, then it is impossible to distinguish between A and B, and nothing can warrant saying that two distinct persons are thinking about the same thing, i.e., emitting the same verbal response. If they are not identical, then it is possible to ascribe one set of descriptions to A and the other to B; indeed, it is precisely the difference in the descriptions of the behavioral responses of A and B that warrants the assertion that A and B are distinct. However, if A and B can thus be said to be distinct, there are no grounds for saying that A and B are thinking about the same p, since the descriptions, 'object of thought of A' and 'object of thought of B' are different.

These examples bring out an interesting feature of non-dualistic ontologies which is also the reason why they give rise to Leibniz's paradox: in a non-dualistic ontology, every predicative relation 'x is y' (i.e., 'x has or possesses y') ultimately reduces to identity, 'x=y'. Thus if mental events constitute the ontological category, the predicative or possessive relation between two apparently distinct categories, 'persons' and 'objects of thought' reduces to the identity of one category: persons= mental events=objects of thought. If 'physical event' is the ontological catgeory, the corresponding analysis is: persons= physical events=objects of thought. But while it is easy to see that the assertion "x and y are identical with z" does not escape Leibniz's paradox, the statement "x and y have the same z" seems perfectly legitimate and non-paradoxical. It is to be noted, however, that "x and y *have* the same z" withstands reduction to "x and y *are* the same z" only if x and y belong to a category which is ontologically distinct from that to which z belongs. There must be an ontological barrier which, as it were, curbs the transitivity of identity which threatens the distinctness of things connected by 'identity'. It is only because of such an ontological barrier between A and B on the one hand and p on the other that the distinctness of A and B from one another remains unaffected despite the sameness of p; or conversely, the object of thought, p, is the same despite the distinctness of A and B. In short, an assertion of identity is non-paradoxical and significant only if a dualistic ontology is assumed.

It is obvious now why the search for a criterion of synonymy and analyticity failed. The search did not fail because it was not carried out conscientiously or far enough but because there was nothing to be found. By denying that meanings are ontologically distinct from observable entities such as linguistic forms or verbal responses, Quine has in effect precluded the possibility that two distinct linguistic forms could have anything in common. It is no wonder then that, except for statements of the form 'A is A' in which the subject and predicate terms are prima facie identical, the supposed relation of synonymy between two prima facie different terms remains unexplained for the simple reason that there is nothing else besides the prima facie terms. Just as it is impossible to show that two distinct physical events are identical, so also it is impossible to show that two distinct linguistic forms are identical or have anything in common. If there is nothing that two distinct linguistic forms can be *shown* to have in common, there is nothing one can do except perform a sort of creatio ex nihilo and *say* that they have, which is essentially what the attempts to establish synonymy by definition or analyticity by semantical rule do. The point is that dualism is required as an ontological basis for the analytic-synthetic distinction and only such a basis can guarantee a genuine possibility of finding a criterion for analyticity.

The attempt to explain analyticity through extensional identity illustrates the necessity for dualism as a basis of analyticity from a different point of view. For this attempt failed not because no criterion was found but because what was found turned out to be empirical and contingent and hence did not qualify as a criterion for analyticity. But it is interesting to note that the reason why a criterion was found at all is that in this case dualism was assumed, namely between the linguistic and the non-linguistic or between words and objects denoted by words. Thus if a criterion of analyticity is to be found at all, a dualism must be assumed between 'language' and something which is neither empirical nor linguistic in the narrow sense in which words or linguistic forms are but which, in Frege's words, exists neither in the inner world of ideas nor in the outer world of things; in short, 'concept' or 'meaning'. Put differently, a non-empirical criterion of analyticity, if there is such a thing, is entrenched in the ontology of concepts or meanings. This shows that, claims to the contrary notwithstanding, the meaning-reference dichotomy which underlies the analytic-synthetic distinction demarcates a division not between language and ontology but between two ontological categories 'meaning' and 'reference'.

The failure of the various proposals to solve the problem of analyticity can thus be traced to the single cause, namely, the lack of awareness of the dualism upon which the problem as well as its solution rests. As a consequence, there are two alternatives with regard to the problem of analyticity: either a dualism must be acknowledged and a criterion of analyticity sought without shunning the intangibles and imponderables entailed by dualism; or if dualism is rejected, the problem of analyticity becomes a pseudo-problem and must be rejected along with the dualism. The fate of the problem of analyticity in the hands of Quine can be illustrated once again in terms of the homely wisdom that "you can't both eat the cake and have it too"; only this time the wise man first swallowed the cake and then proclaimed to others that they can't have it. The traditional notion of 'analyticity' was clouded by mysterious, intangible entities called 'meanings'. Quine wanted to clarify 'analyticity' by disentangling it from such entities and considering it a property of observable, tangible things such as 'linguistic forms'. Instead of appealing to identity of meanings, one is now to look for either identity of linguistic forms or identity of extensions. But as it turned out that 'analyticity' consists in neither of these, Quine concluded that there is no criteria for analyticity to be found and hence no analytic-synthetic distinction to be drawn. It did not seem to occur to him that the notion of 'analyticity' is inextricably bound up with that of 'meaning', and if the latter is intangible and mysterious, so is the former. By eliminating meanings, Quine has precluded the possibility of finding a criterion of analyticity, and it is hardly surprising then that no criterion is actually found.

VI

THE BUDDHIST LOGICIANS ON THE
ANALYTIC-SYNTHETIC DISTINCTION

The Buddhist logicians, like their Western colleagues, argue that conceptual-empirical knowledge is the result of a synthesis, namely the assimilation of different things under the same name or concept. But while the Westerners, including Quine, believe that things and concepts arise from two ultimately distinct and independent sources, experience and language, the Buddhists maintain that these sources are themselves the result of synthesis. A Buddhist might ask Quine where the sources of language and experience in turn lie, and Quine would be hard out to answer without appealing to 'reality' as the ultimate source or ground. For if language and experience are not grounded in reality, they must be grounded either in themselves or in one another. But if language and experience are grounded in themselves and nothing else, then they are the irreducible, ultimate sources; and to say that they are grounded in one another is to admit that language and experience do not constitute two distinct sources of knowledge. The Buddhist logician's point is that the synthesis is prior to these sources as well as the reality in which they are grounded. If it be objected that 'synthesis' implies that there is something prior to the synthesis, namely, those things that are synthesized, the Buddhist answer is that one is not cognizant of those things. The Buddhists have also shown why this is so: the point-instants of reality which are the ultimate ingredients of the synthesis, considered in themselves, do not give rise to cognition of objects; it is the synthesis of the point-instants that results in cognition and therewith conceptual-empirical knowledge. The synthesis consists in being unaware of the absolute dissimilarities of the point-instants, which from the viewpoint of ultimate reality signifies ignorance but from the standpoint of conceptual-empirical knowledge makes possible discrimination and perceptual judgment. Thus, although the point-instant is never the direct object of cognition or perceptual judgment, "the point-instant of reality receives in such a judgment its place in a corresponding temporal series of point-instants, it becomes installed in concrete time and becomes a part of an object having duration [santāna]."[1] It is to be noted, however, that the point-instant does not thereby become a 'source' of knowledge, if by this is meant that there is a cognitive (logical, epistemological, or a priori) link between the point-instants and the things and concepts which are objects of cognition. For 'cognitive link' presupposes cognition and exists only in virtue of cognition, whereas the causal-temporal series of point-instants is not cognized *as* a series of point-instants (prior to synthesis) but only as an object having spatial and temporal extension (after synthesis). Put simply, since sources of knowledge exist only in virtue of cognition and cognition is the product of synthesis, there are no sources of knowledge prior to synthesis.

The Buddhist logicians are thus in agreement with the successors of Kant, including Quine, in that objects of cognition presuppose duration and extension. Concerning judgments about the objects of cognition, the Buddhist view is that "owing again to a special synthesis of these moments it [the spatio-temporal object] gets all its sensible and other qualities and becomes a universal [sāmānya lakṣaṇa = ekatva adhyavasāya]."[2] The Buddhist view thus further parallels the Western and Kantian view that perceptual judgments consist of synthesis of the concrete, particular object and the abstract, general attribute. However, as has been pointed out earlier (pp. 21-22), the Buddhist logicians' account of the origin of spatial extension, temporal duration, and spatio-temporal objects differs radically from that of Kant and other Westerners. Thus Kant regarded space and time as the a priori forms of perception which are the necessary presuppositions of the possibility of cognition of spatio-temporal objects. But if the object is not an a priori form like space and time, it may be asked, what is the origin of the object ? In other words, if the a priori forms of perception are only the necessary condition for perception of phenomenal objects, Kant must explain what the sufficient condition is, and this he cannot do without appeal to the noumenal reality. Aware of the difficulties which Kant had in explaining the con-

1. Stcherbatsky, *Buddhist Logic*, Vol. I, p.213.
2. *Ibid.*

nection between the noumena and the phenomena, most contemporary Western philosophers have refrained from giving any explanations as to the origin of space, time, and spatio-temporal object, and have more or less satisfied themselves with the contention that they are just there. By thus deliberately ignoring the problem, contemporary Western philosophers have not removed its cause, namely the belief that immediate objects of cognition are in principle separate, although in actual experience not separable, from space and time. For the need to account for the origin of something arises when this something is claimed to have an independent reality, a self-sufficient existence of its own. The Buddhists, on the other hand, avoid the problem of explaining the origin of space, time, and object altogether by denying that these have separate existences. According to the Buddhists, space, time, and object are inseparable; there could be no space and time without objects and vice versa, no objects without space and time. All three are mutually dependent and arise simultaneously as result of synthesis of the point-instants. As a consequence, the Buddhists maintain that there is no intrinsic difference between the so-called concrete and particular (unsynthesized) on the one hand and the abstract universal (synthesized) on the other but only degrees of abstraction and a continuous process of synthesis. What appears in cognition as a concrete object is already abstracted through synthesis of the point-instants.

It may be objected, however, that the Buddhist account of 'synthesis' is a theory of the origin or genesis of concepts and things and has therefore little to do with a type of judgments called 'synthetic' which are contrasted with another type of judgments called 'analytic'. Hence, it may be argued, the Buddhist theory should be dismissed as a 'genetic account' which has no relevance to the conceptual problem of the analytic-synthetic distinction. However, it is worth noting that although the Buddhist account is genetic insofar as it traces the origin of concepts in cognition, it does not beg the question as most genetic accounts do. Thus 'genetic account' of concepts usually consists of an explanation as to how concepts have been acquired, learned, or discovered by people, and such an explanation obviously begs the question concerning the nature or status—in this sense 'origin'—of concepts themselves. In contrast, the Buddhist account provides an explanation as to how concepts are formed in the first place, irrespective of how they may be acquired by people. Such an explanation is significant in that it shows that the variety in conceptual meaning and world-views arising out of conceptual meaning is not only due to cultural divergences and the different manners in which concepts are transmitted from one generation to the next, but to the intrinsic nature of concepts themselves as products of synthesis. Thus there are infinitely many ways of synthesizing concepts. To illustrate by way of a metaphor, the point-instant may be regarded as a point of origin and the process of synthesis as a ray dispersed outward from the point. There are then infinitely many paths that a ray may traverse to reach the outer sphere where cognition of objects takes place.[1] It is to be noted that the Buddhist defense of conceptual relativism and theoretical pluralism does not rest merely on empirical observations and inductive arguments but rather stems from an excruciating analysis of the nature of conceptual thought. Thus the Buddhists will argue that were there but one uniform linguistic community in the world, the fixity of conceptual meaning would still be relative and contingent, and if there were but one universal conception of reality shared by all people, this would not, Leibniz's dreams notwithstanding, prove the absolute correctness of that conception; if anything, it would testify to the poverty of imagination on the part of the people.

The foregoing observations show the relative nature of conceptual meaning, which, however, does not amount to showing that there is no difference between analytic and synthetic judgments; the analytic-synthetic distinction may still exist relative to a given linguistic community. One may therefore ask, if synthesis precedes every kind of judgment, how do the Buddhists account for the difference between the judgments "this tree is a śiṁśapā" and "a śiṁśapā is a tree", which in the Western view correspond to synthetic and analytic judgments respectively ? Stcherbatsky has suggested that the difference between these judgments in Buddhist terms consists in the fact that the objects which are synthesized in the former judgment

---

1. This metaphor is borrowed from Stcherbatsky who employs it in a different context to illustrate the relationship between the point-instant and the object of cognition. (Stcherbatsky, *Buddhist Logic*, Vol. I, p. 220).

are *things*, i.e., different śiṁśapā trees or the same śiṁśapā tree at different times, whereas in the latter they are *concepts*, i.e., 'śiṁśapā' and 'tree.' "Thus the term synthetic refers to synthesis of two different things, the term analytic to a synthesis of two different concepts."[1] In Stcherbatsky's opinion the Buddhist dichotomy between analytic and synthetic judgments is just as sharp, if not even sharper, than the Western analytic-synthetic distinction. According to him, while the Western criterion of analyticity (if one is to be found) may admit degrees of analyticity, depending on the state of knowledge, the Buddhist dichotomy is strictly mutually exclusive.[2] It may be noted that in Stcherbatky's characterization of analytic judgments as 'synthesis of different concepts' and synthetic judgments as 'synthesis of different things', the sharpness of the dichotomy rests solely on the distinction between 'things' and 'concepts'. However, it has been pointed out that the Buddhists specifically deny any intrinsic difference between things and concepts; according to the Buddhists both refer to a conceptual construction, and the difference between them is only a difference in the degree of abstraction. It seems to follow, then, that one could say at most that judgments exhibit different degrees of analyticity and that Stcherbatsky is mistaken in thinking that 'analytic' and 'synthetic' refer to exclusive classes of judgments.

On the other hand, the Buddhists do maintain that there are two mutually exclusive and jointly exhaustive classes of inferential judgments, namely, those that are based on Identity and those based on Non-Identity (or Causation). Stcherbatsky's claim that the Buddhists acknowledge the analytic-synthetic distinction is based on this distinction. It will be shown that Stcherbatsky's mistake lies not in thinking that the Buddhists divide all judgments into two mutually exclusive classes but in thinking that the division corresponds to what is known in the West as the analytic-synthetic division.

Thus it is true enough that the Buddhist logicians divide all judgments into two kinds, those based on Identity (Tādātmya) and those based on Causation or Non-Identity.

1. Stcherbatsky, *Buddhist Logic*, p. 256.
2. *Ibid*.

Because, as regards (ultimate) reality, (the entity underlying) the logical reason is either just the same as the
entity (underlying) the predicate, or it is causally derived
from it. In reality, there are only two necessary relations,
Identity and Causation.[1]

From this Stcherbatsky concludes :

Thus the division of all inferential judgments, affirming the
necessary connection, or dependence, of one thing upon
another, their division in those that are founded on Identical Reference and those that are founded on Non-Identical, but interdependent, Reference, is exhaustive, since
it is founded on the principle of dichotomy.[2]

However, whether or not this division corresponds to the analytic-synthetic division depends on the meanings of 'Identity' and
'Reference'. It is therefore important to examine what the
cognitive basis of inferences based on the principle of Identical
Reference (svabhāva anumāna) is; in particular, whether the
principle of Identical Reference constitutes a cognitive criterion
of analyticity. The parallel between what the Buddhists call
'inference based on Identical Reference' and what in the West
is known as 'analytic judgment is close enough. Thus to say
that "a śiṁśapā is a tree" is analytic means that one can infer
from the mere presence of śiṁśapā the presence of a tree. (Similarly, one can infer from 'bachelor' to 'unmarried man'.) Hence,
to ask for cognitive criterion of the analyticity of the judgment
"śiṁśapā is a tree" is to ask on what grounds does one infer 'tree'
from 'śiṁśapā.' The Buddhist answer is that the inference
presupposes the knowledge that 'śiṁśapā' is a variety of a 'tree'.
However, such knowledge involves not only knowing that a
śiṁśapā is a tree but also that some trees are śiṁśapās. Indeed,
without knowing that at least one tree is a śiṁśapā, one could not
know that any śiṁśapās are trees. Thus the synthetic judgment
"some śiṁśapās are trees" is a necessary condition for inferring
"this is a tree" from "this is a śiṁśapā," i.e., for knowing that
the judgment "a śiṁśapā is a tree" is analytic. "Thus the concept

1. Dharmakīrti, N.B., p. 73.
2. Stcherbatsky, Buddhist Logic, Vol. I, p. 273.

of 'svabhāva' does not point only to what is known as the logically analytic proposition. It can apply equally well to what is
logically regarded as an empirical or synthetic proposition."[1]
Stcherbatsky is therefore wrong in thinking that svabhāva
expresses just an analytic judgment and that the underlying
notion of identity (tādātmya) means 'identity' in the strict
sense of the term. Rather, "tādātmya... points to the existence
of two properties in the same thing."[2] Moreover, when one
recalls that the Buddhists deny any ontological distinction between
'things' and 'properties' so that for them every difference between
properties is ultimately a difference between things and vice
versa, it becomes clear that tādātmya results from a synthesis of
two different things (or properties). Therefore tādātmya does
not constitute a cognitive criterion of analyticity, for it does not
form the basis for recognizing that a given judgment is analytic
but rather presupposes such a recognition. The Buddhist point
is that merely staring at a particular object will not enable one
to know that "a śiṁśapā is a tree" is analytic. One must know
that the words 'śiṁśapā' and 'tree' both refer to that object,
and the Buddhists have shown that such knowledge is synthetic.

At this point it may be objected that the Buddhist analysis
has little bearing on the problem of analyticity as formulated by
Western philosophers. For the problem of analyticity is specifically a problem of meaning or linguistic entities, whereas the
Buddhist logicians so far have been concerned exclusively with
reference and therefore have not really addressed themselves to
the problem of analyticity, or at least have failed to treat it
adequately. It is to be noted, however, that such a charge
presupposes that meaning and reference are distinct, whereas
the Buddhists deny that 'meaning' and 'reference' have distinct
origins. On the other hand, if 'meaning' and 'reference' point
to one and the same origin, namely conceptual construction,
as the Buddhists maintain, they must show that their analysis
of the cognitive basis of 'identity' holds regardless of whether
'identity of meaning' or 'identity of reference' is appealed to as
the criterion of analyticity.

1. S. S. Barlingay, *A Modern Introduction to Indian Logic*, National Publishing House, Delhi, 1965, p. 131.
2. *Ibid.*

Thus it may be insisted that one is not supposed to consider the reference but only the meanings of the words 'śiṁśapā' and 'tree' in order to know that the judgment "a śiṁśapā is a tree" is analytic. The Buddhist, however, would now ask, how does one know that the meanings of the words are identical or even that they are in any way related ?—Surely not by merely staring at the words ! The only possible answer seems to be that one knows the identity of meanings by knowing that the reference is the same, and thus the circle is closed: One tries to explain identity of reference in terms of identity of meanings only to find that identity of meaning cannot be explained without appealing to identity of reference. The Buddhists would now point out that the circularity is due to the fact that what is explained and that which explains are not distinct in the first place, and hence the explanation of identity of meaning in terms of identity of reference is as unilluminating as the attempt to explain identity of meaning without appeal to identity of reference is futile and hopeless. The former is like the assertion that perception of color is really perception of extended surface, and the latter like the attempt to show that one can perceive a color without perceiving an extended surface. Both are equally absurd and result from the failure to see that colors and extended surfaces are not distinct realities. Thus, whether one appeals to 'identity of meaning' or 'identity of reference' as a criterion of analyticity makes no difference; the cognitive basis of such appeals is the same. The Buddhists have shown that the ways and methods of knowing that śiṁśapās are trees or that bachelors are unmarried men are essentially not different from the ways and methods of knowing that śiṁśapās are tall or that bachelors are lonely. One does not look for non-empirical, non-contingent criteria in the case of the latter judgments unless one is suffering from a nostalgia for the Platonic world. And the Buddhists have shown that the search for such criteria in the case of the former judgments is nothing but a search for the Platonic world.

It is to be noted that the basis of the Buddhist contention that all judgments are synthetic is their denial of the dichotomy between the analytic and the synthetic and ultimately between meaning and reference. The Buddhist contention is therefore not to be mistaken for the claim that all judgments are reducible to synthetic judgments. For if the latter were the Buddhist claim, they would be implicitly affirming the very dichotomy which they deny. Like all dual concepts generated out of an exhaustive dichotomy, 'analytic' and 'synthetic' are polar concepts, each acquiring its meaning in contrast with the other. Therefore one cannot be affirmed or negated without implicitly affirming or negating the other. In other words, if the dichotomy is abolished, it makes as much (or as little) sense to say that all things are now reduced to one category as it does to say that they are reduced to the other. A case in point is the mental-material dichotomy. Thus some philosophers have been eager to abolish the dichotomy by showing that everything 'mental' can be reduced to 'material', without however realizing that they have thereby prepared the ground for their opponent's thesis that everything is mental; or, insofar as they claim to have refuted their opponent's thesis, they have also undermined their own. Similarly, whereas the reduction of analytic judgments to synthetic rests on the analytic-synthetic *dichotomy*, from the rejection of the dichotomy it follows that every judgment is analytic just as well as it is synthetic—or what amounts to the same thing, it is neither analytic nor synthetic. It is therefore not enough for the Buddhists to show that synthesis is a necessary condition for analysis and the so-called 'analytic judgments', but they must also show that synthesis is a sufficient condition for analysis.

The observation that whatever has been put together by synthesis can be taken apart by analysis is a truism, but it forms the basis for the Buddhist claim that all synthetic judgments are also analytic. From the Buddhist view that all of the so-called ingredients of knowledge, including the immediate objects of cognition, are already products of synthesis it follows that there are no components of knowledge which are in principle unanalyzable. In short, the Buddhists do not admit unanalyzable 'simples' as the basic ingredients of knowledge. Thus in the Buddhist view, not only everything that has been synthesized can be analyzed, but indeed there is nothing that cannot be synthesized and therefore analyzed.

It is interesting to note that
> The same Sanskrit term which has been interpreted....as
> meaning synthesis in a conception means, curiously enough,

also analysis or division in the same conception.   It is a
vox media.   The uniting tie of these both meanings seems to
have been the idea of construction which is also the meaning of the verbal root from which the word is derived.[1]

In contrast, according to most Western logicians, the immediate objects of cognition, whether they are 'physical objects',
'sense-data', or 'values of bound variables',   are regarded as
unsynthesized   and   therefore   unanalyzable   'simples'.   Thus
while the Westerners have no quarrel with the observation that
whatever has been synthesized can also be analyzed, they would
maintain that not everything has been synthesized and therefore
not everything can be analyzed.   It has also been noted (pp.
10, 81) that the admission of one unsynthesized component
(i.e., 'referent') logically compels the admission of another (i.e.,
'meaning'), for the question inevitably arises, what is the unsynthesized component synthesized with ?   Thus both the quest
for a criterion of referent and the quest for a criterion of analyticity
arise out of the same assumption, namely, that the ultimate
objects of knowledge are unsynthesized, unanalyzable simples.
      The doctrine of the unsynthesized, unanalyzable simples
forms the ontological basis for the logical distinction between
subject and predicate.   For the claim that two things are distinct
is really the claim that one cannot be exhaustively analyzed in
terms of the other.   But to say that the subject is distinct from
its predicates is to claim that the subject cannot be exhaustively
analyzed in terms of anything at all; in a word, the subject is an
ultimate simple.   Not surprisingly, the subject-predicate distinction is a necessary condition for the analytic-synthetic distinction. Thus, logically speaking, the distinction between analytic
judgments and synthetic judgments is that between judgments
of identity and predicative judgments. Accordingly, the truth
of the synthetic judgment "bachelors are lonely" depends on
the truth of '(x) (Bx $\supset$ Lx)', whereas the truth of the analytic
judgment "bachelors are unmarried men" does not depend on the
truth of '(x) (Bx $\supset$ Ux)', but on the truth of 'B=U'.
      By the same token, the Buddhist rejection of the doctrine
of unsynthesized simples is the basis of their denial of the subject–

1. Stcherbatsky, *Buddhist Logic*, Vol. I, p. 219.

predicate distinction. As noted earlier, for the Buddhists the subject is nothing over and above its predicates, hence all predicative relations collapse into identity : the subject *is* its predicates. Thus all judgments are analytic insofar as they affirm the identity of subject (object of cognition) and predicate (concept of image). It is to be noted, however, that the identity which according to the Buddhists is affirmed in all judgments is not the same identity which in the Western view forms the criterion of analyticity, namely the identity of two concepts such as 'bachelor' and 'unmarried man'. In the Buddhist view it is not that one first perceives a bachelor and then judges him to be unmarried (or first knows the meaning of 'bachelor' and then judges it to be the same as 'unmarried man') on the basis of a mysterious, pre-existing identity. On the other hand, to maintain, as the Buddhists do, that one cannot judge a bachelor to be an unmarried man without the prior synthetic knowledge that a bachelor is an unmarried man is in effect to say that when one judges a bachelor to be an unmarried man the object of one's cognition is an unmarried man.

The rejection of the subject-predicate distinction implies the rejection of the epistemological claim that x perceives 'sense-data' or 'physical object' which x judges to be, e.g., a flower. What is affirmed by the rejection of the subject-predicate distinction is that x actually perceives a flower (which x judges to be a flower). One cannot but notice the striking resemblance between this view and the position of naive realism. Indeed, for the realist, too, all judgments are analytic insofar as they all affirm the identity between the linguistic object and the extra-linguistic object ! The difference between the Buddhists and the realists concerns their ontological claims. Thus the realist upholds a complete isomorphism between language and reality, which leads him to deny that there is any difference between a linguistic entity and its extra-linguistic counterpart. On the other hand, the Buddhists deny that there is any correspondence between linguistic and extra-linguistic entities, which is to say that there are no extra-linguistic counterparts of linguistic entities. Interestingly enough, this leads the Buddhists also to deny that there is any difference between the so-called linguistic and extra-linguistic objects !

The Buddhists challenge anyone to show how one judges,

or indeed perceives, something to be a flower without possessing the concept 'flower'; or, for that matter, how one can perceive anything at all without conceptualization. The Buddhists are fully prepared to accept the radical consequences of their analysis, namely that our perceptions are verified by our own images, our judgments validated by our own thoughts, and our discoveries are but our own inventions?

> To judge means to deal with one's own internal reflex, which is not an external object, in the conviction that it is an external object. This identification is neither a 'grasping' of an external object by its image, nor a converting of the image into an external object, nor is it a real uniting of two things, nor a real imputation, or placing of one thing in the place of another one. It is our illusion, a wrong imputation.[1]

VII

CONCLUSIONS

Contrary to the position of some Western epistemologists and logicians, both past and present, the basic questions of knowledge are inseparable from questions of ontology. No matter what other beliefs and presuppositions a theorist of knowledge may accept or reject, the one question which invariably confronts him is, what is the relationship between knowledge and that which is ultimately the object of knowledge, in short, between the conceptual and the non-conceptual. At the most fundamental level, there are just two alternatives to choose from: Either one may maintain that both the conceptual and non-conceptual elements are present in knowledge and that the central task of a theorist of knowledge is to explicate and clarify the relationship between them; or one may deny that the non-conceptual element enters into the sphere of cognition and knowledge and hence that one cannot even talk about a relationship between the conceptual and the non-conceptual. The former position affirms ontological dualism, i.e., the view that the conceptual and the non-conceptual constitute in principle distinct sources of knowledge, while the latter view embraces ontological non-dualism, i.e., the denial that there are two distinct sources of knowledge. Most of Western philosophical tradition rests on ontological dualism, while the Buddhist logicians represent ontological non-dualism.

Ontological dualism has given rise to two interrelated doctrines which attempt to explain and clarify the relationship between the conceptual and the non-conceptual in knowledge. These are the meaning-reference and the analytic-synthetic distinctions. The most cogent expression and exposition of these distinctions has been given in recent philosophy by Russell, although their roots are traceable to the Western philosophical tradition in general and to Kant and Frege in particular. In contemporary philosophy, Quine has been critical of the absolutism in ontology implicit in the tradition of Kant, Frege, and Russell and has argued that ontology is dependent on, and varies with, the context of discourse and the goals and purposes at hand, and that choices among ontological alternatives must therefore not be made according to absolute, realistic standards but according to relative, pragmatic standards. Quine's views have led him to attack the meaning-reference and the analytic-synthetic distinctions which are the cornerstones of realist and absolutist ontologies. Quine's criticisms have brought him in many respects close to the Buddhist logicians' position according to which all connections between conceptual and the non-conceptual and therewith the meaning-reference and the analytic-synthetic distinctions are ultimately rejected.

The present work which is an inquiry into the analysis of these problems by the Buddhists on the one hand and by some contemporary Western philosophers, for example, Quine, on the other, has led to the following conclusions.

(1) The Buddhist ontology is a thoroughgoing process ontology, whereas Western ontology is essentially a substance ontology. The differences between the two ontologies result in different solutions to some fundamental philosophical problems which are common to both systems of thought, arising out of the attempt to *describe* what there is. This is not to say, however, that what is deemed as a problem in Western philosophy is necessarily considered a problem in the Buddhist philosophy and vice versa. Thus, for example, the problem of the analytic and the synthetic as well as that of meaning and reference which have been haunting Western philosophy are not serious problems, or perhaps no problems at all, to the Buddhist philosophers. But insofar as it is the very spirit of philosophical inquiry that a philosopher of one school of thought confronts and evaluates the problems of another, the above two problems which are specifically Western are analyzed in the light of Buddhist ontology.

(2) The roots of the problem of the analytic and the synthetic and of meaning and reference have been shown to lie in substance ontology. It has also been noted that implicit in substance ontology is the ontological problem of substance and quality and the logical problem of subject and predicate. It has only recently been recognized in the West that the problems of the analytic and the synthetic and that of meaning and reference are variations of the basic problematic theme of language and reality.

It is a truism that central to any discourse is the concept

of meaning and, more importantly, the constancy of meaning.
For otherwise one cannot even begin to talk. But if an ontology
subscribes to a meaning-reference dualism, then that ontology
necessarily commits itself not only to constancy of meaning
but also to constancy of referent. It is irrelevant what the
referents are thought to be, whether Russell's sense-data, Strawson's spatio-temporal particulars, or Quine's values of bound
variables. The point to note is that meaning-reference dichotomy necessarily commits one to constant referents. And what
are constant referents? They could only be whatever
could be referred to by the same term at different times. But
these are nothing but our old substances. It is in this manner
that substance ontology underlies the various epistemological
dualisms such as the analytic-synthetic, language-fact, meaning-
reference, and subject-predicate.

It is true that as a matter of fact every epistemological
inquiry, without exception, needs and postulates dualisms. But
that is not the Buddhist point. It is rather that the mistake
consists in ontologizing such dualisms, in other words, in thinking
that such epistemological dualisms somehow enable one to get out
of one's epistemological skin and reach toward some supposed
independent reality. According to the Buddhists, all such
attempts are a result of wishful thinking. It may be remarked
here that according to the Buddhists, the above dualisms are
disguised variations of the more primordial dualism at the heart
of all thought, namely, similarity versus difference.

(3) Ever since Kant, an analytic statement is understood
as one which can be certified solely on the basis of an examination of the meanings of its constituent terms; on the other hand,
a synthetic statement is one which cannot be certified on the basis
of meanings alone but which requires an inspection of the word.
It is in this manner that the problem of meaning and reference
is implicit in the problem of the analytic and the synthetic. The
Western philosophical tradition, having accepted the meaning-
reference distinction, has naturally accepted the synthetic-analy-
tic distinction. It is interesting to note that the basis and validity
of these distinctions have rarely been called into question, much
less investigated.

(4) Only recently, in a penetrating inquiry, Quine has
shown that all attempts to explicate and clarify 'analyticity' have

begged the question; that is, they have failed to delineate and justify the concept of 'analyticity' on the basis of independent criteria. If so, Quine has argued, 'analyticity is a self-validating concept and hence cannot be significantly contrasted with the concept of 'synthetic'. In this manner, Quine has shown the analytic-synthetic distinction to be spurious. Put differently, there cannot be any sharp line of demarcation between the analytic and the synthetic. It must be borne in mind, however, that Quine does not deny that one does draw a distinction between the analytic and the synthetic but only that there is no justification for drawing one. He fully grants that, as a matter of fact, the philosopher, the logician, and the scientist do make such a distinction.

(5) A careful study of the Buddhist logicians reveals that they too hold that the analytic-synthetic distinction is unfounded. It has been shown in the present work that the Buddhist rejection of the analytic-synthetic as well as the meaning-reference distinction is due to their rejection of the fundamental dualism, namely the conceptual versus the non-conceptual. This is an important point of difference between Quine and the Buddhist logicians. In sharp contrast with the Buddhist logicians, Quine's arguments against the analytic-synthetic distinction do not stem from the rejection of the primordial dualism of the conceptual and the non-conceptual, but rather consists of an examination of various ways of explicating 'analyticity' and showing that all these ways are vitiated by circularity namely employing the very notion to explicate it.

(6) It is not surprising, then, that there is a glaring inconsistency in Quine's overall epistemological and ontological analyses. Thus while he rejects the analytic-synthetic distinction and therewith the fact-language distinction with respect to individual statements, Quine nevertheless claims that "Taken collectively, science has its double dependence on language and experience; but this duality is not significantly traceable into the statements of science, *taken one by one*."[1]

The reason for such inconsistency and ambiguity in Quine's position seems to lie in the inadequacy of his analysis of the nature of conceptual thought as such. Quine restricts his analysis to certain kinds of conceptual thought, namely those

1. Quine, "Two Dogmas of Empiricism," *From a Logical Point of View*, p. 42 (emphasis added).

that arise out of the Indo-European languages. Thus, contrary to his own claim, Quine accepts without question certain grammatical structures which are characteristic of the Indo-European languages (but not necessarily of all languages), in particular the subject-predicate structure of sentences, and therewith the ontological assumptions underlying such structures—in this case the meaning-reference dichotomy. Quine's ontological relativism which is based on pragmatic criteria paradoxically flourishes within the confines of certain ontological assumptions (second-order ontological statements) which are not themselves relative. This is not surprising, however, for, as has been shown, pragmatic criteria ultimately beg the ontological question insofar as the goals and purposes that set the pragmatic criteria themselves arise out of some ontological presuppositions. There are therefore certain ontological assumptions that pragmatic tests cannot reach but which are self-validating. In Quine's analysis, the second-order ontological statements are such self-validating statements.

(7) The Buddhist logicians' theory of knowledge and reality is quite consistent in that their rejection of the dualism of the conceptual and the non-conceptual automatically leads to the rejection of all other kinds of dualisms, such as the analytic-synthetic and the meaning-reference. But what precisely does the Buddhist rejection of the conceptual versus non-conceptual dualism mean? It certainly does not mean the denial of reality (ontological nihilism), nor does it mean that reality is conjured up and produced by the human mind (subjective idealism). Rather it means that, as far as the enterprise of knowledge is concerned, all objects and entities are conceptual constructions. This is so because, as has been shown, according to the Buddhists, all cognition takes place in some conceptual construction and synthesis or other. This is necessarily so, because the term 'discursive knowledge' has no meaning apart from conceptual constructions. In a word, there can be no talk of the 'given' apart from its being given in some categorial schema or other. It follows from this as a corollary that there can be no talk of reality itself. There can only be different conceptual schemas, different constructions, and different descriptions of what different people *think* reality is. Thus, if all knowledge is shot through with conceptual constructions, it is pointless to talk about going

out of the constructions and reaching for the so-called 'referents'. What counts as a referent is determined by the conceptual schema. As such one cannot, according to the Buddhists, talk about 'meaning' and 'analytic statements' on the one hand and 'reference' and 'synthetic statements' on the other. It should be kept in mind, however, this does not mean that the Buddhists are claiming that all statements are analytic or all statements are synthetic. To think so is to entirely miss their point, which is simply that the whole talk of such dichotomous classification of statements is misguided and unwarranted and could only be a result of either sheer confusion or rigid dogmatism. But no matter which, it points to deep-seated ontological anxiety which is the urge to talk about the untalkable, to capture the non-conceptual through the conceptual. It may be remarked here that, according to the Buddhists, dualistic epistemologies and ontologies and therewith ontological anxiety are nothing but the inevitable result of the efforts at self-transcendence. For, after all, is one not trying to transcend oneself when one asks what the world is like apart from one's conceptions of the world ? —when one in effect demands to know the world apart from one's means of knowing the world ? Is it not the case that the meaning-reference problem arises in one's effort to find the things which one's words supposedly refer to ? It cannot be too strongly emphasized that the central insight of the Buddhists is as illuminating as it is devastating—the insight that all epistemological and ontological enterprises attempting self-transcendence are doomed to failure. In order to prevent any misunderstanding, it may be repeated that the Buddhists are not denying that there is reality, but only that there is an epistemological route to reality which would circumvent the very categories of that route. Needless to mention, for the Buddhists the time-honored Western distinction between epistemology and ontology is nothing short of a fond delusion.

(8) Lest anyone misunderstand the author as recommending that philosophers as well as plebians give up thinking and constructing systems, it is worth emphasizing the main point: There is nothing wrong with constructing conceptual systems, philosophic or scientific as long as one recognizes that every system, actual and potential, is a limited system, if for no other reason than the fact that they are all generated by some

set of dualism or other.   And dualisms are the manifestations
of polarity at the very core of systems; and the virtue, and at the
same time the vice, of polarity are limitation and relativity. Thus
the mistake consists of launching upon the search for some
absolute system, by means of which to grasp that elusive ontological beast with golden mane and silver tail.   By a relentless
analysis of thought and knowledge, the Buddhists have shown
that such ontological excursions are no more fruitful than the
search for gods and dragons.   It is hoped that the present writer
has successfully brought out this point.

ADDENDA AND CORRIGENDA

P. 29. L. 17. Insert the following material between the words "Much" and "Ontological"

of contemporary Western philosophy consists of attempts to reconcile the rift in one way or another.

But neither the concerns of the philosophers of "ordinary language nor those of most other contemporary Western philosophers can be fully understood without recourse to what may be called 'ontological anxiety.' Ontological anxiety results from the gulf between what *can* by philosophical standards (whatever these may be) be considered true and what *is* believed to be true no matter what. Thus the extremely anti-ontological attitudes, such as expressed in the view that philosophers ought to be concerned with words and not with things can be seen as a radical attempt to eliminate the gulf by outlawing what have traditionally been regarded as properly philosophical pursuits. At the same time, however, the persistent preoccupation of the philosophers of "ordinary language" with words—despite their own admission that ordinary men fare much better with words than they themselves—can only be understood as an expression of deep-seated ontological anxiety which cannot be cured by words alone, ordinary or otherwise.

Thus ontological anxiety lies at the root of not only the search for ontological justification which Popper criticizes but also of the opposite attitude which religiously avoids all ontological issues; in short, it underlies and inspires most of the central problems of contemporary Western philosophy. A classic manifestation of ontological anxiety is the attempt to compensate for the loss of

P. 46. L. 21 Read different *for* differnt

P. 53 L. 22 After 'is not thought of' add : as following from a more basic statement, on

BIBLIOGRAPHY

Books

Annambhaṭṭa. *Tarka-Saṃgraha*, commentary by Y.V. Athalye, introduction and English translation by M.R. Bodas. Bombay Sanskrit Series, 55, Bombay, 1930.

Bagchi, S. Inductive Reasoning, *A Study of Tarka and Its Role in Indian Logic*, Calcutta, 1955.

Barlingay, S.S. *A Modern Introduction to Indian Logic*. National Publishing House, Delhi, 1965.

Barrett, W. *Irrational Man* : *A Study in Existential Philosophy*. Doubleday, New York, 1962.

Bergson, Henri. *Introduction to Metaphysics*. Philosophical Library, New York, 1961.

Bochenski, I.M. *A History of Formal Logic*, tr. and ed. Ivo Thomas. University of Notre Dame Press, 1961.

Buddhaghosa. *Visudhi Magga*, ed. Mrs. Rhys Davids, 2 Vols. The Pali Text Society, London, 1920-21. Selected translations by Warren, Henry Clarke, *Buddhism in Translations*, Atheneum, New York, 1963.

Bradley, F.H. *Principles of Logic*. Oxford, 2nd ed., 1922.

Carnap, Rudolph. *Meaning and Necessity*: *A Study in Semantics and Modal Logic*. University of Chicago Press, Chicago and London, 1964.

Cohen, M.R. and Nagel, E. An Introduction to *Logic and Scientific Method*. Harcourt Brace and Company, New York, 1936.

Conze, E. *Buddhism. Its Essence and Development*. Oxford, 1951.

——. *Buddhist Texts Through the Ages*. Oxford, 1954.

Dasgupta, S.N. *A History of Indian Philosophy*, Vols I and II. Cambridge, 1922 and 1932.

Davidson, D. and Hintikka, J., eds. *Words and Objections*. *Essays on the Works of W.V. Quine*. Synthese Library, D. Reidel Publishing Company, Dordrecht-Holland, 1969.

Dharmakīrti. *Nyāya-bindu*, tr. Th. Stcherbatsky, Buddhist Logic, Vol. II, Dover Publications, Inc., New York, 1962.

——. *Pramāṇavārttikam*, ed. with notes by R. Gnoli. Serie Orientale Roma, XXIII, Rome, 1960.

Dharmottara. *Apoha-Nāma-Prakaraṇa*, Tibetan tr. in the Tan-
    guyr: Mdo Zo, India Office Library, folios 254-256.
——. *Nyāya-bindu-ṭīkā*, ed. Th. Stcherbatsky. Bibliotheca
    Buddhica, VII, Leningrad, 1918. English translation
    with notes by Th. Stcherbatsky, *Buddhist Logic*, Vol. II,
    Dover Publications, Inc., New York, 1962.
Dīgha-Nikāya, ed. T.W. Rhys Davids and J.E. Carpenter, 2 Vols.,
    Pali Text Society, London, 1890-1911. Tr. by T.W.and
    C.A.F. Rhys Davids, *Dialogue of the Buddha*. *Sacred
    Books of the Buddhists*, Vols. 2, 3 and 4, Oxford University
    Press, London, 1899-1921.
Dignāga. *Nyāyamukha*, ed. Giuseppe Tucci. Heidelberg (Leib-
    zig) 1930.
——. *Nyāya-Praveśa*, ed. with notes by Anandshankar B. Dhruva.
    Baroda, Oriental Institute, 1930.
——. *Pramāṇasamuccaya*, ed. H.R. Rangaswamy Iyengar.
    University of Mysore, 1930.
Hegel, G.W.F. *Hegel's Phenomenology of Mind*, tr. William
    Wallace. Clarendon Press, Oxford, 1894.
Hiriyanna, M. *The Essentials of Indian Philosophy*. George
    Allen & Unwin, Ltd., London, 1932.
——. *The Indian Philosophical Studies*. Mysore, 1957.
——. *Outlines of Indian Philosophy*. George Allen and Unwin,
    Ltd., London, 1932.
Husserl, E. *Formal and Transcendental Logic*, tr. Dorion Cairns.
    Martinus Nijhoff, The Hague, 1969.
Ingalls, D.H.H. *Materials for the Study of Navya-Nyāya Logic*.
    Harvard Oriental Series, 40, Cambridge, Mass., 1951.
Jayatilleke, K.N. *Early Buddhist Theory of Knowledge*. Allen
    & Unwin, Ltd., London, 1963.
Kant, Immanuel. *Critique of Pure Reason*, tr. N. Kemp Smith,
    abridged ed., Random House, New York, 1958.
Keith, A.B. *Indian Logic and Atomism*. Oxford, 1921.
Klemke, E.D. *Essays on Frege*. University of Illinois Press,
    Urbana, Chicago and London, 1968.
Korner, S. *What is Philosophy?* The Penguin Press, London,
    1969.
Leibniz, G.W.F. *New Essays Concerning Human Understanding*,
    tr. A.G. Lanley, Lasalle, Illinois, 1949.

Majjhima Nikāya, ed. V. Trenkner and R. Chalmers, 3 Vols. Pali Text Society, London, 1948-51. tr. I.B. Horner, *Middle Length Sayings*, 3 Vols., Pali Text Society, London, 1954-59.

Matilal, B.K. *The Navya-Nyāya Doctrine of Negation. The Semantics and Ontology of Negative Statements in Navya-Nyāya Philosophy.* Harvard University Press, Cambridge, Mass., 1968.

McKeon, R. *The Basic Works of Aristotle.* Random House, New York, 1941.

Murti, T.R.V. *Central Philosophy of Buddhism. A Study of the Mādhyamika System,* Allen & Unwin, Ltd., London 1953.

Nāgārjuna. *Aṣṭasāhasrika Prajñāpāramitā* (The Perfection of Wisdom in Eight Thousand Ślokas). Bibliotheka Indica, Work No. 284, Issue No. 1578, Calcutta, 1958.

——. *Mūlamādhyamakakārikās de Nāgārjuna avec la Prasannapada,* Commentaire de Chandrakīrti, ed. Louis de la Vallee Poussin. St. Petersburg, 1913. Tr. Frederick Streng, *Emptiness. A Study in Religious Meaning.* Parthenon Press, Nashville, Tennessee, 1967.

Nakamura, Hajime, *Ways of Thinking of Eastern Peoples, India, China, Tibet and Japan,* ed. Philip Wiener. East West Center Press, Honolulu, Hawaii, 1964.

Pandeya, R.C. *The Problem of Meaning in Indian Philosophy,* Motilal Banarsidass, Delhi, 1963.

Plato, *Collected Dialogues of Plato,* ed. E. Hamilton and H. Cairns. Pantheon Books, New York, 1961.

Popper, Karl R. *Conjectures and Refutations.* Basic Books, New York, 1962.

Potter, Karl H. *Presuppositions of India's Philosophies.* Prentice Hall, Inc., New Jersey, 1963.

Quine, W.V. *From a Logical Point of View.* Harper Torchbooks, New York, 1963.

——. *Ontological Relativity and other Essays.* Columbia University Press, New York, 1969.

——. *Word and Object.* M.I.T. Press Cambridge, Mass., 1960.

Radhakrishnan, S. and Moore, C.A. *A Sourcebook in Indian Philosophy.* Princeton University Press, New Jersey, 1957.

Raja, Kunjunni, K. *Indian Theories of Meaning.* The Adyar Library Research Center, 1963.

Ramanan, K.V. *Nāgārjuna's Philosophy as Presented in the Mahā-prajñāpāramitā Śāstra*, Varanasi-1. India, 1971.

Randall, J.H., Jr. *Aristotle*, Columbia University Press, New York, 1962.

Ratnakīrti. *Apoha-Siddhiḥ*, tr. with commentary by D. Sharma, *The Differentiation Theory of Meaning in Indian Logic*. Mouton & Co., Printers, The Hague, 1969.

———. *Kṣaṇabhaṅgasiddhiḥ Vyatirekātmikā*, ed. with introduction, translation and notes by A.C. Senape McDermott, *An Eleventh Century Buddhist Logic of 'Exists'*. D. Reidel Publishing Company, Dordrecht-Holland, 1970.

———. *Ratnakīrti-Nibandhāvalī*, ed. with introduction by Anantlal Thakur. Tibetan Sanskrit Works Series, Vol. III, Kashi Prasad Jayaswal Research Institute, Patna, 1957.

Russell, B. *An Inquiry into Meaning and Truth*. Allen & Unwin, Ltd., London, 1956.

———. *Human Knowledge, Its Scope and Limits*. Simon & Schuster, New York, 1962.

———. *Logic and Knowledge*, ed. R.C. Marsh. The Macmillan Company, Great Britain, 1964.

———. *The Problems of Philosophy*. Galaxy Books. Oxford University Press, New York, 1960.

Ryle, G. *The Concept of Mind*. Hutchinson's University Library, London, 1949.

Saṁyutta Nikāya, ed. L. Feer, 6 Vols., Pali Text Society, London, 1884-1904. Tr. C.A.F. Rhys Davids and F. Woodward. *The Book of the Kindred Sayings*, 5 Vols., Pali Text Society, London, 1917-30.

Sastri, S. Kuppuswami. *Primer of Indian Logic* (with translation of Tarka-Saṁgraha of Annambhaṭṭa), The Kuppuswami Sastri Research Institute, Madras, 1932.

Sesonske, A., ed. *Plato's Republic : Interpretation and Criticism*. Wadsworth Publishing Company, Inc., Belmont, California, 1966.

Stace, W.T. *The Philosophy of Hegel*. Dover, New York, 1955.

Stcherbatsky, Th. *Buddhist Logic*, Vols. I and II, Dover Publications, Inc., New York, 1962.

———. *The Conception of Buddhist Nirvāṇa*, Leningrad, 1927.

Vācaspati Miśra. *Nyāya-vārttika-tātparya-ṭīkā*. Benares ed.

1925. Tr. by Th. Stcherbatsky, *Buddhist Logic*, Vol. II, Dover Publications, Inc., New York, 1962.

Vidyabhushan, Satischandra. *A History of Indian Logic. Ancient, Medieval and Modern Schools.* Calcutta, 1921.

Wittgenstein, L. *Tractatus Logico-Philosophicus*, Routledge and Kegan Paul, London, 1961.

White, M. *Toward Reunion in Philosophy.* Atheneum., New York, 1963.

Whorf, B. *Language, Thought and Reality.* London and New York, 1956.

Articles

Bahm, Archie J. "Does Seven-Fold Predication Equal Four-Cornered Negation Reverscd," *Philosophy East and West*, Vol. 7, pp. 127-30.

Brough, J. "Logic," *Encyclopaedia of Religion and Ethics*, Vol. 8, pp. 127-32.

Chatterji, Durgacharan. "Sources of Knowledge in Buddhist Logic," *Indian Culture*, Vol. VI, Nos. 1-4, July 1934, April 1935, pp. 263-73.

Datta, D.M. "The Source of Primary Negative Judgments," *The Proceedings of the Indian Philosophical Congress*, 1929.

Dharmottara, "Kṣaṇabhaṅgasiddhiḥ, tr, into German by E. Frauwallner, *Wiener Zeitschrift fur die Kunde des Morgenlands*, 42, 1935, pp. 217-58.

Frege, Gottlob. "The Thought : A Logical Inquiry," tr. in *Mind.*, July 1956, p. 301.

Friedman, D. "Aspects of Indian Epistemology, Logic and Ontology," *Philosophia Reformata*, Kampen, 1955.

Heineman, F.H. "The Meaning of Negation," *The Proceedings of* the Aristotelian Society, No. 8, Vol. XLV, 1943-4, pp. 127-52.

Jayatilleke, K.N. "A Recent Criticism of Buddhism," *University of Ceylon Review*, Vol. 15, pp. 135-50.

——. "Factual Meaning and Verification," *University of Ceylon Review*, Vol. 13, pp. 1-16.

Kitagowa, Hidenori, "A Note on the Methodology in the Study of Indian Logic," *The Journal of Indian and Buddhist*

Studies, Vol. VIII, No. 1, University of Tokyo, January 1960, pp. 380-90.

Kunst, A. "The Principle of Excluded Middle in Buddhism," *Roeznik Orientalistyczny*, 21, 1957, pp. 141-7.

Puligandla, R. and Puhakka, L.K. "The Challenge of the Absurd," *Journal of Thought*, Vol. 5, No. 2, 1970, pp. 101-11.

Raju, P.T. "The Principle of Four-Cornered Negation in Indian Philosophy," *Review of Metaphysics*, Vol. 7, pp. 694-713.

Rhys Davids, C.A.F. "Logic (Buddhist)," *Encyclopaedia of Religion and Ethics*, Vol. 8, pp. 132-3.

Robinson, R.H. "Some Logical Aspects of Nāgārjuna's System," *Philosophy East and West*, Vol. VI, No. 4. University of Hawaii Press, January 1957, pp. 291-308.

Sharma, D. "Epistemological Negative Dialectics of Indian Logic—Abhava versus Anupalabdhi," *Indo-Iranian Journal*, Vol. IX, No. 4, 1966.

——. "The Paradox of Negative Judgment and Indian Logic." *The Vishveshvaranand Indological Journal*, Vol. II, Part 1, March 1964.

Staal, J.F. "Formal Structures in Indian Logic," *Synthese*, Vol. XII., No, 43, September 1960, pp. 279-86.

——. "Means of Formalization in Indian and Western Logic," Proceedings of the XIIth International Congress of Philosophy, Vol. X, Paris 1958, Firenze 1960, pp. 221-7.

——. "Correlations between Language and Logic in Indian Thought ? A Comparative Study," *The Bulletin of the School of Oriental and African Studies*, Vol. XXV, Part 1, University of London, 1962, pp. 52-71.

GENERAL INDEX

absolute, 5
absurdity, 6-7
Adhyavasyati, 49
ākaram, 49
analytic
—and synthetic, 10, 60-64,
72-73, 84, 86-90, 93-96
—statements, 63, 72, 83, 85
analytical deduction, 13-14, 24
analyticity, 10, 65-74
—criteria for, 10, 64, 65-74,
79, 85, 86-90
—problem of, 10, 61, 65-80,
83, 87
apoha, 46, 51
apohavāda, 46
Aristotle, 3, 28, 57

being, 2, 3, 4
behavioristic explanation, 17
bergson, 21
bound variable, 37, 39, 53,
56, 90, 94

causation, 85, 86
cause, 22, 23
cognition, 23, 49-52, 81, 82
Cohen, Morris, 4
comparative studies, iv, 8
Cratylus, 1-2

denotation, 35
denote, 33
descriptions, 16, 17, 41, 57, 58
—Russell's theory of, 32,
33-36
dharma, 55
Dharmakīrti, 7, 19, 20, 50
Dharmottara, 7, 52
differentiation, 46, 49, 51-52
—theory of meaning, 46, 59
Dignāga, 7

double standard of reality,
7-8, 20
dualism, 61-62, 72, 74-79, 93,
97, 99, See also ontological
—generic, 62, 63
dualistic, 58, 59, 63, 98
duovocalism, 29
duration, 21, 82

existence, 21, 22, 23, 83
existential quantifier, 17-18,
33, 56
extension, 21, 22, 69, 82

Frege, G., 58, 76, 93

Hegel, 5
Hume, 15-16
hypostatization, 14

idealism, 97
ideas, 76
—of external world, 15-16
—Plato's theory of, 2-3, 54
identity, 10, 17, 45, 75-79,
85, 86, 87
—criterion of, 10
—law of, 4, 28
—operator, 33, 34
ignorance, 25, 44
—of particular object, 44
—primordial, 44
illusion, 25, 26, 44, 92
inherence, 55, 58

Jung, Carl, 45
justification, 15, 18-19, 58, 59

Kant, 5, 48, 82, 93
knowledge, 7, 34
—Buddhist theory of, 25-27
—by acquaintance, 35, 49